P9-DTV-282

LANGUAGE AND THOUGHT IN SCHIZOPHRENIA

Language and Thought in Schizophrenia

COLLECTED PAPERS PRESENTED AT THE MEETING OF THE AMERICAN PSYCHIATRIC ASSOCIATION, MAY 12, 1939
CHICAGO, ILLINOIS

Edited by J. S. KASANIN, M. D.

With a Preface by NOLAN D. C. LEWIS, M. D.
FORMERLY PROFESSOR OF PSYCHIATRY, COLUMBIA UNIVERSITY MEDICAL SCHOOL, AND DIRECTOR, NEW YORK STATE PSYCHIATRIC INSTITUTE AND HOSPITAL

The Norton Library
W · W · NORTON & COMPANY · INC ·
NEW YORK

First published in the Norton Library 1964 by arrangement
with the University of California Press

Published simultaneously in
Canada by George J. McLeod Limited, Toronto

ISBN 0 393 00252 7

W. W. Norton & Company, Inc. is also the publisher of
the works of Erik H. Erikson, Otto Fenichel, Karen Horney and
Harry Stack Sullivan, and the principal works of Sigmund Freud.

PRINTED IN THE UNITED STATES OF AMERICA

7 8 9 0

Preface

NOLAN D. C. LEWIS, M.D.

IN ORDER to detect and understand psychopathological features appearing in thought and language, it is desirable, if not actually necessary, to know as much as possible about the average or normal construction and functions of these important characteristics of man. Language is probably the most momentous and most baffling product of the human mind—a phenomenon that is handed down by social inheritance from generation to generation. Discordant opinions with respect to the basis and superstructure of language organization are still vying for favor among scholars who have studied the subject for years and are well versed in the facts of language history. It is yet far from clear just how the facts accumulated can be coördinated and explained.

All students are agreed that language is the expression of human thought. It is "natural to man." From the highest civilized peoples to the most belated primitives, all men speak in some fashion and are able to interchange such thoughts as they possess. Moreover, man is the sole possessor of language as such. A certain degree of power of communication, sufficient for the comparatively restricted needs of their gregarious intercourse, is displayed also by many species of the lower animals; but these types of response are not only greatly inferior in their degree to human language, they are also so radically diverse in kind that the same name cannot with justice be applied to both.

Language in the sense in which it serves as the subject of the studies comprising this monograph is one of the most conspicuous and fundamental of the characteristics of man. It is a very complex affair, composed of various orders of the signs of thought. In the broadest sense it might include, besides audible signs of thought such as words and sentences, all other ways of communication—gestures, postures, facial expressions, and so on. If language is but the instrument for the expression of thought, it then comes to be just what the users make it.

As speech is observed in everyday life, it is a congeries of individual languages differing with the intellectual capacity, the training, and the experience of the person using it. Every language used by a people has its own characteristic framework of established distinctions, its shapes and forms of thought into which, for the one who learns that language as his "native tongue," are cast the contents of his mind, his mass of acquired impressions, and his knowledge of the environment. This is brought about as a result of external influence; it is imposed from without, and is associated with the process by which the individual acquires the material of expression itself. It is not a product of his free, undirected internal forces; his mind has been led to view things and to group them in certain ways and to contemplate them consciously in those particular relations.

The structure of even the most elaborate languages, rich in expressions, embodies and brings to consciousness or awareness only a small part of the great wealth of relations existing among the objects of thought and recognized impliedly, within, although no attention is directed to them by expression.

Although man possesses various faculties and capacities which integrate in a manner allowing for and leading inevitably to the production of thought and speech, these capacities are one thing and their elaborated complicated products are another. Men are not born artists, engineers, or speakers, but are made so, in large part, by their human contacts. Language is a type of social action which was developed by man in his relations with other men. The aim and function of the verbal expression is the transmission of some thought or feeling pertinent to the moment and in the midst of a present situation. Utterance and situation are bound up intimately with each other, and the meaning of the situation must be known for the words to be understandable. Thus language is a function of the situation and must be so interpreted if an investigator is ever to approach and understand such things as unconscious motives.

The language of the emotions is not rich in expressions, at least not particularly in those at present well understood. The "physiology" of language is difficult enough to comprehend, and its "pathology" outside of a few well-studied organic conditions has hardly been tapped.

Words are symbols which are used in different patterns and levels of meaning. Their significance must be ascertained by a thorough study of their functional roles; and this is just what the researches reported in this book have attempted to do in the mental disorder known as schizophrenia.

A thorough study of language and other behavior phenomena constitutes the most fruitful approach to the study of thought in schizophrenia as well as of other mental disorders. The language of schizophrenic patients has commanded the attention of psychiatrists and of other students because of its curious distortions. They often use words and sentences the meaning of which is not familiar to the normal or average person. Many if not most of these words are peculiar to the patient and usually have a special significance. The language of schizophrenics may have a formal but involved structure that accomplishes little in interhuman communications. Thus, they are alleged to have "labyrinthine minds," or they may express themselves in a "word hash" having no apparent articulated structure.

The various clinical expressions of the well-established schizophrenic process seen daily in the mental hospitals have been interpreted by almost all experienced psychiatrists as indicating a profound disturbance of thought and language. Among those presenting features repeatedly emphasized in this connection are fundamental or fancy-born inconsistencies more or less foreign to normal or average conscious life; shut-in tendencies, with a sense of something wrong or unusual going on in the environment; indulgence in vague artistic fantasies, with daydreaming and partial withdrawal from reality, or at least lack of concentration on the tangible realities of the present life situation; automatic and dissociated thought processes, often with projection as ideas of reference and active hallucinations; content disorders, with self-reference, with feelings of being hypnotized, the mind being read, or made to do things against the will or desire; odd mental influences, with transformation experiences; grotesque incongruities of judgment, with accounts of fantastic episodes; scattering of thought and speech, with curious condensations and complaints of unnatural interference with thought, combined with oddities of statement and fantastic action; impulsive episodes and vagueness, with shifts of emotional reactions; responses with opposites and "word hash," or with other evidence of marked disorganization in language such as neologisms and distortions of content.

To the problem of schizophrenic thinking, several types of approach have been made. The disturbances of association are the basic symptoms emphasized by Bleuler, who considered the schizophrenias in the plural. The associations become weak and disconnected. Owing to this weakness, the affects gain "dominion over the train of thought" and "wishes and fears control the trend instead of logical connections"; thus delusions are formed, often dominating the ideational content, and marked dereistic thinking obtains, with its disregard for ordinary logic and its tendency to symbolism, displacement, and condensation. Dereistic thinking is pleasurable thinking, or it may resemble that of dreams, falsifying reality. Bleuler considered condensation to be promoted by the incompleteness of ideas. He also spoke of the "displacement" of ideas as due to one idea's appearing for another, and of the symbol as a special form of displacement taking the place of the original idea.

Fragmentary and otherwise disturbed associations may render the speech of the schizophrenic illogical or even unintelligible although in the mind of the patient the ideas behind it may be connected. This phenomenon is particularly prominent late in the disorder or when a serious disorganization of the personality has occurred, although either loose or involved thinking or odd sequences of ideas are not infrequently noted in the prepsychotic life of the person.

Brevity of associations leads to so-called "impoverished" thinking, and "blocking" occurs when the associations approach painful conflict material. Preoccupation with affective factors is alleged to be the principal cause of a poverty of associations. The mental stream is thus disturbed by obstructive thoughts and by thought pressure, and there is often the symptom of perseveration on words or topics. A tendency to generalizations is also a conspicuous trait; but these generalizations are often so vague that they have no meaning for the average person. Many abstract words lacking in precision are used, and metaphorical expressions are not uncommon.

Affective elements are held to account for the ellipses, neologisms, and odd ideas which are the condensations and symbols of conflict situations. Although schizophrenic thinking resembles the prelogical thinking of children and of primitive people, both types seeming to be paralogical in nature, there is some question whether these phenomena indicate or should be called "regression." So far, this depends entirely upon the definition of regression offered by the observer.

Kraepelin and Bleuler and their students, with accurate, detailed descriptions of the behavior of schizophrenics, revealed a fruitful field for subsequent investigators, who have proceeded along one or another of a number of different lines of approach, devising concepts and methods aimed toward a better understanding of the psychic interior of the patient. Among these approaches are the genetic, the neurodynamic, the neurophysiological, the neuropathological, the psychological testing, and the phenomenological descriptive varieties, each based on one or more of the different constellations of features of schizophrenic thought and language. Multiple approaches have some value, so long as the synthetic attitude is maintained.

The mind of man is an incredible complex of impressions, transformations, and productions, the meanings of which are not easy to determine. Under certain conditions it becomes notably disordered, and we desire to know the nature of these conditions, what factors enter into them, and how best they can be understood and corrected. This monograph presents data accumulated from material analyzed from different points of view, with some synthesis and interpretation of results provided by recent investigations in the whole field having to do with the subject of thought and language in schizophrenics. If some of the present interpretations engender doubt and contradiction among fellow investigators, so much the better for our science; for where discordance is active, there the most favorable and even essential conditions for progress are present.

Contents

Introductory Remarks

J. S. KASANIN, M.D.

SCHIZOPHRENIA is the most baffling disease in psychiatry, if not in all medicine. Intellectual impairment and a striking disturbance of the emotional life are the chief features of this disease. The whole concept of schizophrenia, or of its more limited manifestation of dementia praecox, postulates an intellectual deterioration. It was this ultimate dementia, or at least intellectual impairment, which made the Kraepelinian classification of mental disease unassailable, since ultimate deterioration was the basis of the classification.

The problem of dementia has always aroused the curiosity of the psychologist dealing with language and thought processes, and the intellectual disturbances in schizophrenia have usually been interpreted in the light of current psychological theories. Until recently, little has been done to learn the exact nature and the cause of this deterioration, partly because experimental techniques are of comparatively recent origin in psychology. In the days of Wundt, we spoke of disturbances of associations in schizophrenia as being due to a break in synaptical continuity or to some other equally obscure cause. It is only in the last century, with the development of experimental psychology, the technique of measurements of intelligence, and especially the experimental methods of genetic and *Gestalt* psychology, that a better understanding of schizophrenic thinking has been attained.

A fine beginning in this field was made by Bleuler and Storch, but after World War I formal investigations in the field of schizophrenic thinking were stopped for almost two decades because of the extreme interest of the psychiatrist in the dynamic aspects of psychiatry as expressed in the teachings of Meyer, Freud, Jung, and others. These investigators pointed out that schizophrenic speech utterances have a definite meaning and content even though they may be quite distorted and incomprehensible to the observer. Although the interest in dynamic psychiatry delayed minute investigations of schizophrenic thinking, it suggested a sound basis for later investigations by pointing out the importance of content in schizophrenia—an emphasis which we owe largely to the teachings of Adolf Meyer. With this stimulation, and with the development of new experimental techniques in psychology, a great deal of investigation was begun in the late 'twenties and 'thirties in Germany, Russia, and the United States. Kurt Goldstein, studying the effect of brain injuries on intellectual functions, made the important observation that with anatomical damage the personality and the whole intellectual grasp of the individual changes. At the same time, in Germany, von Domarus began to study the laws of logic in schizophrenia, and the Russians, Luria and Vigotsky, applying certain experimental techniques of genetic psychology, developed a very ingenious method of studying impairment of thinking in schizophrenia. In addition to the work of these psychiatrists, the important methods of the so-called "personality tests" were being applied to the problem of schizophrenia.

I have mentioned that the first experimental research in schizophrenic thinking was delayed because of the attempt of psychiatrists to understand in dynamic terms the nature of a schizophrenic's psychosis. However, there has gradually developed something of an understanding of why and how a psychosis develops, and of what the schizophrenic tries to say in the words he utters. One of the greatest students of schizophrenia, and one who combines unusual knowledge with extraordinary intuition, is Dr. Harry Stack Sullivan, whose contribution is the first in the present symposium.

The Language of Schizophrenia

HARRY STACK SULLIVAN, M.D.

THE PROBLEM of language and thought in schizophrenia has interested me for many years. Man's first experience, birth, is schizophrenic. As he grows older, the time comes when he has to accommodate himself to the language of his people and take on their language. Everyone takes on language from those who are immediately available to provide it, those whom we might call culture carriers.

Why do all of us develop language behavior? The development is necessary because without language people cannot function. The way language is acquired is extremely important to any understanding of those peculiarities which have been described as the "unpsychological" aspects of schizophrenia. People acquire language because culture—any culture—that has endured for centuries is now so complex that as soon as one can he must begin to live in an unreal world, unreal because it is shot through with subtle evaluations.

Fairly early in one's extrauterine existence one has to operate with the term "I." This term is, I believe, properly included in the interesting category of pronominal things. Because everyone is lonely and in need of any encouragement that can be obtained from his environment, he is taught to take nourishment, to take air, to adjust himself to his physical environment; this requires practical movements. When we come to deal with the terribly significant people who seem to be intimately related to social environment, we realize that the sooner we become skillful in operating in terms of a pronominal existence the better. The more skillful we become in this complex linguistic activity, the more often do we get what we want and the fewer are the disappointments we experience. We learn quite early in life that our parents can always *refer* to themselves, and we learn to refer to ourselves. Thus begins the development of that system of experience which we call the "self system," the organization of successful tricks, mostly linguistic, by which we conciliate others and get as much satisfaction as we can.

Throughout life, language is largely an instrumentality for getting what we want. As we live with other human beings, we are creatures of culture; and as linguistic culture is the most amazing of all cultural ingredients, linguistic symbols—speech—are very important instrumentalities in our getting what we want. So inadequate is the structure of our culture to our needs that language operations have to pertain not only to obtaining what we do want, but also to saving us from experiences, both real and imaginary, which we do not want.

Getting what we want is, generically, securing satisfaction; avoiding what we do not want is the preservation of our feeling of personal security. Most children learn to use language more to preserve security than to secure satisfaction. It is an inevitable inference from the very nature of culture that high cultural abstractions pertain more to the feeling of personal security among our fellows than they do to biological satisfactions.

Freud, who has been able to penetrate to very broad generalities in his *Civilization and Its Discontents,* says that civilized behavior arises from repression of the sex instinct. Now I would not wish to make that generalization the keystone of all future developments in the theory of knowledge, but I would suggest that anything that can have attracted Freud's attention and passed his tests and come forth in a generalization of that simplicity is a very important insight into the structure of human life. When he says that civilized behavior arises only from the repression of the sexual instinct by social demands, he is touching upon much the same thing I have in mind when I say that the child, from the appearance of the capacity to integrate certain types of behavior (which really are exquisite refinements of the laryngeal and pharyngeal instrumentalities) so that articulate speech becomes possible, uses language and linguistic phenomena very largely to preserve his feeling of security among his fellow men.

Many of you who have a more direct contact with life than I have may feel that I am mistaken in this appraisal of language behavior. You believe that at least since mid-adolescence you have used language in the pursuit of certain types of satisfactions. You may be right. On the other hand, you may have been careless in your observations. Speech certainly precedes some satisfaction-giving activities. For that matter, speech precedes, interlaces, and follows almost every interpersonal relation. And pronominal "I" is quite ready to take it very seriously with respect to its effects on the situation.

All language operations are, in a certain sense, magical. That is a dangerous generalization; there is nothing of mysterious power about language, and there are language operations, for example those of the mathematician, which show no trace of magic but which formulate inevitable relations between sets of facts preferably extremely abstract. If the facts are not extremely abstract, this "perfect" use of language is difficult or impossible. Most language operations are magical in the sense that they are supposed to color powerfully the complex woof of events which involve one, the warp of which is, very largely, the thread of impersonal change. In other words, one follows the pervasive weavings of one's thoughts and arrives somewhat unexpectedly in error, whereas the related events, impersonal or interpersonal, still move on after their own fashion.

The peculiarities of language behavior in the schizophrenic arise from his extreme need of a feeling of personal security. The schizophrenic, early convinced that since it is unobtainable, satisfaction is not the prime consideration of life, uses language exclusively and more or less knowingly in the pursuit of durable security. A durable feeling of personal security is practically impossible because culture has not been organized to provide it, since all cultures evolve from certain irrational premises of human beings—not only irrational, but pathetically inadequate. Thus all cultures thus far evolved are irrational and include impossible contradictions. Since language is the most subtle and powerful lever that any culture provides, most linguistic operations of human beings in general, and all linguistic operations of the schizophrenic, have to be oriented toward the pursuit of something quite impossible of attainment: a feeling of security in the presence of strangers. As the schizophrenic, because of the very insecurity which has always characterized him, has tended even more to divorcement from these fellow men with whom he has never felt secure, the language operations at the height of a schizophrenic episode show most perfectly the sheerly magical operations which men effect by language.

The "unpsychological" aspect of schizophrenic living is, I insist, chiefly a misinterpretation of the schizophrenic's verbal magic in a world of verbal entities.

Can we find any correlative to this peculiarity of the schizophrenic? It was my great good fortune on one occasion to be profoundly fatigued while in the presence of friends with whom I felt secure. On this occasion, since one of my friends was an almost intolerable bore when on the subject then being discussed, I fell asleep. I was trying to be a good social animal at the time I fell asleep.

I was, in fact, engaged in telling a story. I was awakened by hearing some most extraordinary solecisms with which I had finished the story. At that time I, at last, after many years of exposure to schizophrenic language, understood what I presumably had known, in some sense, for many years.

Language operations as thought are profoundly different, quite fundamentally different, from language operations as communication and as pure mechanisms used in dealing with others; the more completely one becomes self-centered, the more utterly he becomes cut off from integrations with other more or less real people, and the more utterly novel, perfectly magical, and wholly individual become the symbols which he uses as if they were language.

Although a teacher of English may use certain phonetic combinations as the perfect English language, all the agreed, authoritative, and demonstrably useful systems of phonetic combinations disappear when he is falling asleep—or when he is thoroughly schizophrenic.

What takes the place of these systems may be suggested by this story. One of my godchildren is precocious and linguistic. When about two, he beguiled one of his parents into promising him a pony. I visited them shortly after this promise had been made. I am interested in horses, and I listened to the conversations. It took me a very short time to realize that what this boy meant by the pony he was going to get was like no pony I had ever known or any that his parents contemplated. This pony was a great thing, such as we could scarcely anticipate or comprehend.

In a word, language always starts as an entirely autistic performance. We hear our parents utter certain phonetic combinations and they appeal to us in terms of the situations in which we hear them. If, for example, one hears "mamma" only when suffering from rebuff, "mamma" for a long time in one's life has an extraordinarily unpleasant connotation. If, however, one hears "mamma" only as an aftermath to the disappearance of all tension, then "mamma" for a long time will have many of the attributes which we later associate with the perfection of heaven. We all start out with a highly individuated language, a set of purely autistic phonetic combinations.

When one is able to relax all vigilance against one's fellows, language similarly regresses toward its beginning. We do not need to become primitive in order to become simple. The safer we are with our fellows, the simpler and also the more autistic becomes our operation with language symbols. This is so much so that very old friends say singularly unimportant words to each other and understand each other perfectly. It is even said that husbands and wives often understand each other without much speech.

When we attack the problem of schizophrenic thinking, we come again upon something which can be understood only by explanations in terms of culture in general and of individual genesis of personality. Vicissitudes of our later academic careers often convince us that language and thought are very intimately related, and it is true that there are thoughts which are related to language. If I prepared an outline of this article, you might profit therefrom; this in itself demonstrates that there is some relationship between language and thought. Nevertheless, the persistent superstitions which one encounters concerning the use of language in thought and the value of language because of its capability of expressing thought seem to me dangerously misleading.

I have for years contemplated the experiment of having a child taught one language for speech and another for writing. This would be quite feasible, although some persistent attitudes make us inept teachers. Such an individual would probably think as well as, if not better than, most of us do. He would not be misled about the intimate relation of language to thought. The fact that one or the other of his languages happened to decorate as grace notes what was going on in his mind would be to him clearly irrelevant. Thinking pertains not to language, but to memory. The relationship of language and thought is both more indirect and more immediate than is ordinarily realized.

We remember a vast series of instantaneous states of our organism, and when we think in complete security and with no strong integrating tendency at work we have nothing like language processes going on in our minds. We have almost nothing "in mind." Certain recollections of past states of the organism flow and shift with extreme velocity to certain things which according to the old psychologists are associated with them, and we arrive at a realization that the intended action, for example, would fail; that is that. Then we begin again and presently we arrive at a series of hypothetical events which might work; and *then* we think. We think in various ways. The most striking way in which we think is how to tell our thoughts to somebody else; if you think of anything in terms of how to tell it to a stranger, your mental process approaches the characteristics of good written language. If the person concerned is, on the other hand, an intimate friend, the mental process gets nowhere near good written language; you now make indicative use of words, use words as signs with which to attract your friend's attention to corresponding experience.

Thinking, so far as I can discover, is the final refinement of the reverie processes by which we meet life. The refinement is largely the reference to other people as potential hearers. In the schizophrenic, this reference to other people is always tenuous. The rest of us rarely experience schizophrenic mental processes, not because they are not there, but because they are not reasonable and are therefore disturbing.

Since we are clinical psychiatrists, our subject is the vicissitudes of language in the hands of schizophrenics. I have been trying to suggest to you that there is nothing different in the phenomena of schizophrenic speech and phenomena historically familiar to each of us in linguistic learning and linguistic performance, that the closest approaches to schizophrenic speech in your daily life occur when you do not need to be alert, because you are secure. The schizophrenic has given up any hopes of satisfaction and is concerned only with the maintenance of security. He shows, often with painful chagrin in retrospect, the autistic type of speech which is probably our second nature, and which we certainly show among our intimates, when we are very tired and safe. I diagnose schizophrenia by certain types of disturbance of speech unaccompanied by chagrin, but I have yet to see a schizophrenic early in his illness who has not been chagrined by hearing himself say certain things to me which he recognized afterwards as incommunicative.

This brings me to the last idea that I wish to present.

The beauty of written language and, in some degree, the charm of spoken language consist not in anything inherent in linguistic processes or language symbols, but in the fact that in our learning of language, in our observance of language behavior, and in our successful formulation of foresights to impress if not to intimidate our teachers, our wives, and our friends, we are depending on that group of processes which I call "consensual validation."

You may take this phrase and divide it: "con" means "with," "sensual" means "state of mind," and "validation" stands for "demonstrating truth." "Consensual validation" might then be agreement between two persons, or among a group, that something is true. That is what it does mean, with a qualification.

It is in this consensual validation that the schizophrenic fails, and from its absence he comes to manifest pathognomonic symptoms. Some grasp of the processes of consensual validation is absolutely necessary in considering any phase of language behavior.

If I speak to an audience, I have a fantastic auditor, almost entirely an invention of my personality, who attends to what I say, notices the more grievous absences of verbs for subjects, prods me gently, as it were, so that I diligently operate this complex neuronic and muscular apparatus in an attempt to say, first, complete sentences; second, sentences of good grammatic structure; and third, good logical sentences. This supervision on the part of a fantastic but realistically constructed auditor is the process of consensual validation.

The last thing to be noted of the disturbances of language processes in the schizophrenic comes from the fact that, being rather unsocialized, undeveloped personalities, these mythical observers who watch over the speech of the schizophrenic are as immature and undeveloped and tortured as the schizophrenic himself. Therefore, what seems to him an adequate verbal expression is likely not to impress its meaning upon us. Of course, there are many nonschizophrenic people, also, who are not entirely out of this class.

The schizophrenic's critic, his observer of speech, shows the same fugitive integration that is so striking in the personal relationships of schizophrenics. The critic passes, as adequate, expressions which are neologistic, is thereby shocked to alertness, and reviews them with chagrin or fear. This is no help to adequate speech.

To summarize, the schizophrenic does not have our pleasant illusions that speech will help him to satisfactions, because he is quite sure there are none. He uses speech exclusively for counteracting his feeling of insecurity among other people. The schizophrenic's speech shows characteristic peculiarities because of recurrent severe disturbances in his relationships with other people and the result is a confusion of the critical faculties concerning the structure of spoken and written language. Some of these peculiarities may be described as regressively related to the speech of very young children, but I hope that no scientist will be so careless as to say that speech and thought in schizophrenia are regressive.

DR. KASANIN:

Dr. Sullivan in discussing the personality aspects of language has pointed out the magical use of language in schizophrenia and the artistic quality of language as a series of phonetic combinations. The more secure we are, the more simple and more artistic is our operation with language symbols. The primary purpose of language—communication—is so impaired in the schizophrenic that his language becomes highly individualistic and can be understood only by those closest to him and those who have a deep understanding of him. In this connection, one must remember that words and ideas expressed by a man do not necessarily convey his real feelings and that one must be able to detect this in speech. Without this intuition on the part of the observer, all language is quite incomprehensible and misleading. This is of the greatest importance in studying language and speech. We find that words, sentences, utterances frequently are a mask for something which the speaker does not wish to disclose.

The great intimacy of schizophrenic speech can be appreciated only by very few. Comprehension probably does not depend upon intuition alone, and obviously the speech must follow certain laws of construction.

Disturbances of speech and language, however, are not observed in schizophrenia alone; they are also observed in organic diseases, in various toxic states, and in brain injuries. For many years before and immediately after World War I, Dr. Kurt Goldstein and his associates made most painstaking studies of brain injuries. They utilized the technique of *Gestalt* psychology because they found out not only that language and certain functions of language were disturbed in brain injuries, but that the whole organism was changed by the injury to the brain, no matter how focalized it might be.

With this rich experience in brain injury, Dr. Goldstein and his assistants applied their technique to the study of the intellectual functions of schizophrenia, and their research is of utmost importance in throwing some light on the relationship of organic brain disease to schizophrenia.

Methodological Approach to the Study of Schizophrenic Thought Disorder

KURT GOLDSTEIN, M.D.

I BELIEVE that progress in research in schizophrenia will come by use of the same methodological procedure that is characteristic of the reorientation of psychopathology in general (5, 6, 10).[1] The new approach is no arbitrary new theory; on the contrary, it has developed necessarily from analysis of observations recorded of patients with organic brain defects. The older orientation in psychopathology tended to explore the individual symptoms or syndromes by themselves; the more recent one regards each phenomenon in relation to the individual as a whole. It is the problem of the total personality of the patient, as it faces us in its bodily as well as its mental aspects, that has come to occupy the center of scientific interest. The symptom is no longer considered simply as a consequence of a defect, but also as an expression of the tendency of the organism to come to terms—in spite of its defect—with the outer world in the best way possible under the given condition.

[1] Numbers in parentheses refer to References Cited on pp. 38–39 below.

From experiences with patients having cortical lesions there has been derived a special methodological procedure which has proved suitable to the study of the change of behavior as a whole: the application of certain sorting tests (*Zuordnungs* tests). This method has revealed that we have to distinguish between two kinds of human behavior, the abstract and the concrete, and that a definite change in behavior, an impairment of abstract behavior, is characteristic of patients with cortical lesions (5, 16).

These attitudes, or behaviors, are not acquired mental sets or habits of an individual, nor do they represent specific aptitudes such as memory or attention. They are, rather, capacity levels of the total personality, each furnishing the basis for all performances on a certain plane of reference to the outer world situation.

The concrete attitude is realistic. In this attitude, we are given over and bound to the immediate experience of the given thing or situation in its particular uniqueness. Our thinking and acting are directed by the immediate claims made by one particular aspect of the object or situation in the environment.

In the abstract attitude, we transgress the immediately given specific aspect or sense impression; we abstract from particular properties. We are oriented in our action by a more conceptual viewpoint, be it a category, a class, or a general meaning under which the particular object before us falls. We detach ourselves from the given impression, and the individual thing represents to us an accidental sample or representative of a category. Hence this attitude is also called the categorical or conceptual attitude. The abstract attitude is basic for the ability:

1. To assume a mental set voluntarily.
2. To shift voluntarily from one aspect of the situation to another.
3. To keep in mind simultaneously various aspects.
4. To grasp the essential of a given whole; to break up a given whole into parts and to isolate them voluntarily.
5. To generalize; to abstract common properties; to plan ahead ideationally; to assume an attitude toward the "mere possible," and to think or perform symbolically.
6. To detach our ego from the outer world.

The abstract behavior is the more active; the concrete, the more passive. The above-mentioned potentialities are not prerequisite for concrete behavior.

We have to differentiate between various degrees of both abstract and concrete behavior. There are various degrees of abstract behavior corresponding to the degree of complexity which the performance in question involves. For instance, an especially high degree of abstract behavior is requisite for the conscious and volitional act of directing any performance whatsoever and accounting for it to oneself or to others. A lesser degree of abstract behavior is required for conceptual behavior if unaccompanied by awareness of one's own doing. Symbolic or metaphoric thinking and behavior in everyday life may be considered as a special instance of the latter behavior.

This gradation applies also to concrete behavior. The most concrete way of dealing with situations or things is to react to but one of their properties, which alone is experienced; for instance, reacting to one color or a particular form of an object, or to the practical use to which the object may be put. A less concrete approach is indicated when the person is embracing in his scope the total concrete configuration of an object or situation and is not determined in his response by one particularity of it alone.

The normal individual combines both attitudes and is capable of shifting from one to the other at will according to the demands of the situation. Some tasks can be performed only by virtue of the abstract attitude; for others, the concrete attitude is sufficient.

In the pathology of patients with brain lesions, behavior is disintegrated in such a way that the capacity for abstract behavior is impaired: the individual is more or less reduced to a level of concreteness and can only perform those tasks which can be fulfilled in a concrete manner (5, 6).

In order to avoid misunderstanding, it is necessary to emphasize that the process of distintegration in the direction of concrete behavior does not prevent the arousal of ideas and thoughts; what it actually affects and modifies is the way of manipulating and operating them. Thoughts do arise, but they can only become effective in a concrete way: just as the patient cannot deal with outer-world objects in a conceptual frame of reference, so he deals with ideas simply as things which belong to an object or situation. Concepts, meanings, categories—other than situational means-end relations—are not within his scope.

Once this was taken into account, many known symptoms of organic cases became better understandable, and many new ones were disclosed which had remained hidden to the older approach. There was special value here for research in aphasia and agnosia.

I think that research in schizophrenia has to take a similar route and that the language and thinking of schizophrenics will become comprehensible only when we appreciate the patient's total behavior change. Vigotsky (18) was the pioneer who adopted our general concept and methodological procedures in his attempt to determine the fundamental mental change in schizophrenia. He, too, used for his studies a sorting test, a modification of a test devised by a psychologist, N. Ach. This test, now named the Vigotsky test, became known in this country through the publications of Kasanin and Hanfmann (14, 15). Vigotsky believed the change he found in schizophrenics to be similar to the impairment of the attitude toward the abstract which we have found in organic cases. Being inclined to attribute the change to an impairment of the thinking process, he spoke of an impairment of "thinking in concepts." Kasanin and Hanfmann have confirmed Vigotsky's findings on a greater number of patients and have tried to place the Vigotsky test on a quantitative basis. Because, in my opinion, this personality change does not concern thinking alone, I prefer to speak of a change in the total behavior and to consider the impairment in thinking a special expression of the latter.

I see with satisfaction that Hanfmann, in one of her latest publications, on the basis of a very careful examination of a case of schizophrenia, agrees with me that "the reduction of loss of the categorical attitude [which her patient showed] is to be considered not as a change within the intellectual sphere alone, but as a basic disturbance in the functioning of the total organism. The intellectual and the emotional disturbance are probably only two manifestations of the one basic change." Cameron, confirming the findings of Hanfmann and Kasanin, comes to the conclusion that "the schizophrenic's tendency to maintain the concrete attitude" is strong (3).

Notwithstanding the usefulness of the Vigotsky test for investigation of schizophrenics, I favor those tests which we introduced for examining irreversible organic cases and those which my co-workers and myself have subsequently developed and improved. These tests seem to me much simpler than the Vigotsky test and therefore more easily given to patients. They are in part described in earlier papers of Gelb's and mine, and of our students in Germany. In this country, the tests have been used in studies of my co-workers, Bolles and Nadel, and of my own. A detailed description of all these tests has been published by Scheerer and myself (8). According to the studies of Vigotsky, Kasanin, Hanfmann, and of Bolles and myself (1, 2), there is no question that *a very great concreteness is characteristic* for the behavior of schizophrenics—at least, of one group.

Many of the peculiarities of the behavior of schizophrenics become understandable when considered as expressions of this abnormal concreteness. Concrete behavior means that in our behavior and activity we are governed, to an abnormal degree, by the outer-world stimuli which present themselves to us, and by the images, ideas, and thoughts which act upon us at the moment. Symptoms arising from this attitude are autistic thinking and acting, and there is an abnormal boundness to outer-world stimuli so far as they belong to that realm of reality which the patient experiences. The world of the schizophrenic is determined to a pathological extent by his own feelings and thinking, and by his capacity to react. The demarcation between the outer world and his ego is more or less suspended or modified in comparison with the normal. Here is one origin of illusions. The objects which impress the patient are not the same as those which would impress the normal person in the given situation. He experiences only objects to which he can react in the only way of which he is capable, that is, in the concrete way. He does not consider the object as part of an ordered outer world separated from himself, as the normal person does.

Hanfmann's description of a case of schizophrenia (13) contains a great number of examples which show that the patient is bound to reality as he experiences it, in a pathologically concrete way. Like our patients with irreversible organic lesions, Hanfmann's patient was unable to "make an unreal assumption or to accept a fictitious situation as such, whether it was expressed in a sentence, a story, or a picture." Because of being limited to this concrete behavior, the patient reacted in the "ball and field" test with the declaration that she had not lost a ball; and in the object-sorting test she placed the fish with the vegetables because "fish goes with pumpkin." Also, the reactions of Hanfmann's patients in the Healy completion test show the pathological boundness to "reality." The schizophrenic always picks out blocks with pictures which show a concrete relation to that part of the picture which he experiences at the moment. Another expression of this attitude is that the patient usually considers the people in the picture as in the process of performing a definite action. To him they appear as moving or pointing to something which is often contrary to the actual situation in which they are presented in the picture.

The reality which belongs to the concrete attitude is more dynamic than static. The patients have a marked tendency to do something. (If an individual is abnormally attracted by the activity of another individual, he will not, of course, be aware of the fact that his behavior does not correspond to the "real" situation.) In the same way, the schizophrenic prefers situations of activity. Objects are experienced as things for definite use. Here, as well as elsewhere, personal attitudes often come to the fore in the same way as in the reactions of the organic patients. The patient puts a horse in the room because "there is a boy, and the boy wants a horse; he wants to travel." He completes pictures according to similarity or equality in the same way as organic patients with impairment of the abstract attitude do in the sorting test, that is, according to a concrete relation, and especially according to use. He says, "I see three boys, and so I put one more with them. It should be all boys, boys, boys." The patient's relation to time also definitely shows the concrete character. A schizophrenic patient of Hanfmann's said, "Eight-thirty is the time to get up" or "the time when the sun goes down." These answers are of exactly the same type as those of organic patients. One of my patients, on being asked what time it was, said, "It must be after 4 o'clock because 4 o'clock is teatime." Another patient said, "It is 12 o'clock because at that time my friend leaves the room, and he is leaving now."

This concreteness also finds its expression in the language of schizophrenics. Analysis reveals that many of the very strange words which the patients use become understandable when considered in relation to the concrete situation which the patient experiences at the moment and which he wants to express in words. In their language there is an absence of generic words which signify categories or classes. Or when they do use such words, analysis shows that for the patient they do not correspond to generalizations. We found the same true of amnesic-aphasic patients.

The concreteness in the language of schizophrenics is especially evident in the investigations made with our tests. For instance, in the color-sorting test one of our patients picked out various shades of green, but in doing so he named them as peacock green, emerald green, taupe green, bright green, equet green, bell green, baby green. He refused to say that all might be called green. Another patient said, in the same situation, "This is the color of the grass in Virginia, this is the color of the grass in Kentucky, this is the color of the bark of the tree, this is the color of the leaves." The words these patients use in naming color belongs to a definite situation in which the individual color is experienced by the patient. The color names do not, as in normal persons, represent the category to which the individual color belongs, but merely represent an individual property of an object. The words have become "individual" words, that is, words which fit only a specific object or situation. This individual character of the word is characteristic of the language of schizophrenics, in general. According to the specific way in which the patient experiences a certain object or situation, a definite property or aspect of the object or situation becomes the basis for the choice of words. This explains why a patient (described by Tuczek) called a bird "le song"; the summer, "le warm"; the cellar, "le spider"; the physician, "le dance" (because "during rounds the physicians skip around the professor"). One of my patients said, instead of mouth, "kiss." A word when used by a schizophrenic appears as part of an object or a situation, not as a representative of it, in the same way as it is used by some patients with irreversible organic diseases. Cameron recently pointed out this concreteness of the schizophrenic's language (3).

These peculiarities of language have erroneously been considered as expressions of symbolic or metaphoric thinking. I agree with Storch (17), who correctly stressed that symbolic thinking belongs to higher forms of thinking which are usually impaired in schizophrenia, and that the observable phenomena are understandable from the point of view that we are dealing with a very concrete form of thinking. Symbolic thinking might incorrectly be suggested because the "physiognomic" aspect which corresponds to a concrete attitude often plays a great role in the schizophrenic's attitude toward the world. The average person, too, is able, and at times inclined, to experience and to see things in such a way that the concrete, dynamic, and expressive qualities overshadow their objective properties; he then speaks of "screaming colors," a "soft" or "harsh sound," an "inviting atmosphere," a "cold look," and the like. When we use the term physiognomic in this connection, we borrow the name from the sphere of facial expressions, and we apply it to all kinds of immediate sensory experiences. The reactions of the schizophrenic are to a high degree determined by this physiognomic concreteness. For example, the patient mentioned above calls the physician "le dance" because during rounds the interns skip around the professor. At first this expression sounds strange, but it becomes understandable from the point of view of concrete physiognomic realism. One other example is very illuminating in this connection. A schizophrenic patient of Storch's suffering from persecutory delusions casts anxious glances at the moving door and exclaims: "Da fressen mich die Türen (There the doors are going to eat me up)." Obviously, the opening and the closing of doors were concretely experienced as the physiognomy of the opening of the mouth of an animal, and therefore had a threatening character. There is no question that the physiognomic character of an object changes greatly with the varying attitudes of the person toward the world and that it also depends largely upon the ideas which govern the individual at the given moment. This fact may account for the impressive variety in the schizophrenic's physiognomic experiences and the peculiar words he uses.

We can grasp the meaning of an individual word only if we know the concrete situation in which it belongs for the speaking person. In schizophrenia it is really very difficult to find out the particular concrete situation to which a word spoken by the patient belongs. If we succeed in finding out, much of the awkwardness in the comprehension of the schizophrenic's language will disappear; his language will become understandable, particularly when we bear in mind that many of the experiences of the schizophrenic differ so widely from those of a normal individual that the ordinary channels of verbal expression are neither sufficient nor suitable for verbalizing these experiences. This is all the more true because language in general in our civilization is more stereotyped and not rich in words to express the specificity of concrete situations. The patient is thus forced to build up a language which, though it may appear strange to the normal person, is adequate for his experiences. But this makes communication between the patient and the physician, so far as it is based on language, very difficult.

The application of the tests mentioned will advance us in understanding the schizophrenic's thinking and speaking because it will help us to discover the special concrete situations in which the patient is living. It is often difficult or impossible to find out in direct conversation or in the investigation of isolated capacities something about the ideas, the hallucinations, and the feelings which govern the patient's behavior. During the execution of the performance tests these factors come into the foreground adventitiously, incidentally, without conscious intent on the part of the patient. It is characteristic of the impairment of the abstract attitude that the subject is not able to give himself an account of what he is doing, and so it is but natural that he is incapable of communicating his inner experiences by spontaneous description. However, these inner experiences may become manifest in his concrete actions because here they belong to the situation and arise without deliberate effort, of which the patient is deprived by his pathologic condition.

The greater concreteness of the patients is the one congruency of behavior in schizophrenia and in cortical lesions which the new approach has disclosed. Here I would point out at least one other similarity. As I have explained elsewhere (11), the modification of performance in organic cases becomes understandable if we consider it, in addition to being a sequel of a distortion of certain capacities, as a behavioristic change corresponding to the functioning of parts of the nervous system which have become isolated from the whole through anatomical defect. The function of isolated parts is changed in a definite way, following definite rules. By recognition of these rules of change in functioning, many of a patient's symptoms become understandable in a unitary way. These modifications represent the positive symptoms, segregated many years ago by Hughling Jackson from the negative symptoms, the symptoms directly produced by the destruction of structure.

Careful observation of patients with organic lesions has disclosed to us some forms of change characteristic of the condition of isolation (11). May I point out some of those characteristics? The thresholds of excitability are changed, and the patients are forced, in a more or less compulsive way, to respond to any stimulation; there is an abnormal instability and rigidity of the reactions (9); there are, especially, signs of disorganization of the normal figure-ground relation. One sequel of isolation is the abnormal concreteness, and the concomitant phenomenon of the impairment of abstract behavior. Phenomena described in schizophrenics as weakness of the capacity of concentration, *Gedankenabreissen,* rigidity and distractibility, forced responsiveness to singularities, contamination—all these and other phenomena we observe in the same manner in organic patients as in schizophrenics, and we can understand them in the same way as phenomena of isolation.

It would lead me too far, to elaborate on the form of isolation peculiar to the nature of schizophrenic pathology. I should like to mention only some examples which may illustrate the influence of that isolation. If a schizophrenic says, "Everything I think of always gets away from me," or "Everything in me is changing continually," or complains, as one of Storch's patients did, "My thoughts are so confused, everything is wavering, nothing is fixed—one cannot hold fast to anything," we are faced with the phenomenon of instability.

If a patient, besides his complaint about the changing of all experiences, also reveals a great fixation to certain events, we meet a phenomenon very well known in organic cases. I have tried to explain that the distractibility and abnormal fixation are expressions of the *same* functional change under various conditions. If another patient says, "One does not know what is coming, one is completely powerless," we are faced with the same abnormal bond to stimuli which is a characteristic symptom of organic cases (7).

Loss of constancy and definiteness in the conception of the structure of objects is equally characteristic of schizophrenic and of organic patients. In organic patients this loss is produced by an impairment of the normal figure-ground formation. Healthy organization of the outer-world experience is based upon our ability to differentiate between those aspects which are essential in a given situation and those which are not. The first aspects are in the foreground of perception, thinking, action, as "figures." What is not essential at the moment is in the "background." This organization is based upon two activities: one, we abstract from the many aspects which may arise at the moment; the other, we have to supplement relations which are not phenomenally present. Both demand the abstract attitude. Any impairment of the capacity for abstraction disturbs the normal discrimination between the essential and unessential in the given situation, between figure and ground. When, for instance, the glass of a window appears as the essential part of our experience, rather than the wall or the frame, or, in other words, when the glass is the figure and the wall or frame is the ground, it is because the "significance" of the window at the moment is represented by the transparent glass. Yet, what we really experience is much more than that. Although we perceive the frame, the color, the dirt spots on the glass, and even encounter some obstacle to our vision in that the glass may obscure the distinctness of the outer world, we need pay no attention to all these unessential phenomena. We immediately place the glass, or the objects which we perceive through the glass, in the foreground. This is determined by the significance of the transparency of the glass for the total situation at the moment. This normal way of experiencing presupposes a definite attitude of the individual toward the world. If we should pay attention to all the various phenomena, without such differential emphasis, then the character of the window would disappear, the glass would no longer be the figure, and the sharp boundaries on which our ordered world is based would lose their precision and our world would be in confusion.

This does occur in organic disease and in schizophrenia. Cameron observed that a "most striking characteristic" of the schizophrenic patients was their "inability to maintain adequate boundaries." Owing to this deficient figure-ground formation, objects or situations which can be grasped as concrete objects come abnormally into the foreground, and, correspondingly, the patient gives an answer which appears, to the normal person, to be a defective recognition. Many illusions and delusions of schizophrenics originate in this way. We must appreciate the vagueness of the boundaries between figure and ground in such patients—the inversion, that is, the coming into the foreground of the ground instead of the figure, and the sudden and nearly permanent fluctuation between figure and ground—if we are to understand many symptoms. One of the most apparent symptoms is an indefiniteness or disappearance of the normal boundaries between the ego and the outer world, which finds its expression in many utterances and actions of the patients. It is more difficult to disclose the origin of these symptoms in schizophrenics than in organic patients. The "normal" world to the schizophrenic is not simply reduced, as it is in organic patients, but is changed according as his ideas change; phenomena enter his perception and determine for him a recognition about which we know nothing. Hence it is difficult to understand his behavior.

As an example of the change from the normal relation between figure and ground, I like to quote the following utterance of a patient of Fischer's: "The air is still here, the air between the things in the room, but the things themselves are not there any more" (4). This defective organization of figure and ground can bring inappropriate objects, or aspects of them, into the foreground and so deprive the patient's world of its normal constancy.

I have to confine myself to these few illustrations. I think that from the point of view here advanced many strange symptoms in schizophrenics become intelligible. We can understand them as reactions which are commensurate with the changed world of the schizophrenic, a world which is pathologically concrete and void of abstract interpretation. This point of view takes into consideration the "formal" change in the process of schizophrenia. Though I emphasize this point, I do not overlook the problem of why on the basis of this defect sometimes one and sometimes another idea comes into the foreground. That, however, is a problem with which we cannot deal here.

In stressing the similarities between the behavior modifications in schizophrenics and organic cases, I do not wish to be misunderstood as considering schizophrenia simply an organic disease. From my general position regarding the body-mind relationship, I am inclined to assume that equivalent functional changes can be produced by organic, that is, structural or chemical changes, as well as by mental derangement. I cannot discuss this problem here. (See 11, p. 336.) I should like only to point out that we may consider the modifications of performance in schizophrenics and in sufferers from organic disease as being equivalent with respect to the change in function. To draw conclusions regarding the possible identity of the underlying processes would, however, be premature. The fact that in both cases there are—besides the similarities—essential differences, should make us cautious.

For lack of space, I can mention here only a few characteristics which might be suitable for demonstrating, in principle, these differences. Let me exemplify them by the difference in impairment of the abstract attitude in either pathological state.

The level and type of concreteness in schizophrenia is not identical with that in somatic cases. The somatic case exhibits a disintegration toward the concrete which is of a simplified and inane form. The situation of the schizophrenic is quite otherwise, because of his different type of concreteness. This is well evidenced, for example, in the performance, with my block test, of both types of patients. In the somatic cases the outstanding deficiency in reproducing the model with the blocks consists in the difficulty of breaking down the configuration and in the determination of the procedure by the simple perception of the given configuration. The type of error committed is quite consistent with the somatic's simplification, and is thus understandable.

The schizophrenic's performance suffers from similar deficiencies, but in addition to his perceptual concreteness the schizophrenic develops his own pattern in grouping the blocks because his personal ideas enter and influence the performance. This introduces an entirely different aspect, since the grouping of the blocks represents a projection of his personalized thinking and associations aroused by the presented models. Since the latter vary continually, the types of error are much less consistent and more individual. This is related to the fact that the world of the schizophrenic is much richer and more animated with personalized ideas than is that of the somatic patient. That the personality change in schizophrenics expresses itself on a different level of concreteness can be seen from another important symptom, namely, from the aforementioned prevalence of the so-called physiognomic aspect of percepts.

It should be clear from these examples that we are dealing with intrinsic differences in the concreteness of the schizophrenic and the somatic. The problem, of course, demands further scrutiny, but it seems to me that the characteristics outlined above tend to show that a closer investigation and comparison of these two features can offer deeper insight into the nature of schizophrenia.

Earlier, there was much discussion of primary and secondary symptoms in schizophrenia: of a fundamental, primary change, and of secondary phenomena which are to be considered as psychological reactions to the primary personality change—that is, as expressions of the struggle on the part of the pathologically modified psyche with the demands of the environment. The primary change was considered either as a somatic nucleus, as a consequence of which bodily and mental symptoms appear (for example, the catatonic phenomena or the disturbances of associations); or it was conceived as being a mental change (for example, an insufficiency of mental activity, intrapsychic ataxia or split personality, and so on).

The clinical picture of schizophrenia contains symptoms which may suggest an origin in a disturbed function of some apparatus of the brain, particularly of the frontal lobes and the subcortical ganglia, and also symptoms which are better interpreted as psychological reactions. Because of the similarity between the defect in abstraction discussed above and the defect found in somatic patients, one might be inclined to assume there is a primary somatic change in schizophrenics. However, the greater concreteness of schizophrenics might also be considered as a way out of the organism's unbearable conflict, a protection against the danger of severe catastrophe. (See 11, p. 35.) Many a symptom found in "organic" as well as in psychogenic diseases is intelligible from this point of view. As yet, it is not possible to arrive at a definite decision whether, in impairment of abstract attitude in schizophrenia, we are dealing with a primary or a secondary phenomenon. I should like to add that a secondary phenomenon may be fixated in such a way that it has the same effect as a primary change as long as there is no possibility of removing it. This is of great relevance to therapy. (See 10, p. 276.)

I think the value of the new methodological approach can be appreciated from what I have said here, even if I have given only fragmentary exemplification. This approach seems appropriate for emancipating from speculation the research on the schizophrenic's thinking and language, and to put it on the sound basis of empirical investigation. We are only at the beginning of such research. The new approach seems to me as promising as it proved in organic psychopathology.

REFERENCES CITED

1. Bolles, M. "The Basis of Pertinence," *Arch. Psychol.*, No. 212 (1937), p. 52.
2. Bolles, M., and K. Goldstein. "A Study of the Impairment of 'Abstract Behavior' in Schizophrenic Patients," *Psychiat. Quart.*, 12 (1938), 42–65.
3. Cameron, N. "Deterioration and Regression in Schizophrenic Thinking," *Jour. Abnor. and Soc. Psychol.*, 34 (1939), 265–270.

4. Fischer, F. "Raum-Zeit-Struktur und Denkstörung in der Schizophrenie," *Zeitschr. f. d. ges. Neurol. u. Psychiat.*, 124 (1930), 246.
5. Goldstein, K., and A. Gelb. "Ueber Farbennamenamnesis," *Psychol. Forsch.*, 6 (1924), 127 ff.
6. Goldstein, K. "The Problem of the Meaning of Words Based upon Observations of Aphasic Patients," *Jour. Psychol.*, 2 (1936), 301.
7. Goldstein, K. "The Modifications of Behavior Consequent to Cerebral Lesions," *Psychiat. Quart.*, 10 (1936), p. 586.
8. Goldstein, K., and M. Scheerer. "Abstract and Concrete Behavior," *Psychol. Monogr.*, Vol. 53, No. 239 (1941).
9. Goldstein, K. "The Significance of the Frontal Lobes for Mental Performances," *Jour. Neurol. and Psychopath.*, 17 (1936), 27–40.
10. Goldstein, K. "The Significance of Psychological Research in Schizophrenia," *Jour. Nerv. and Ment. Dis.*, Vol. 97, No. 3 (1943).
11. Goldstein, K. *The Organism: A Holistic Approach to Biology Derived from Pathological Data in Man* (New York, American Book Company, 1939).
12. Goldstein, K. *Aftereffects of Brain Injuries in War* (New York, Grune & Stratton, 1942).
13. Hanfmann, E. "Analysis of the Thinking Disorder in a Case of Schizophrenia," *Arch. Neurol. and Psychiat.*, 41 (1939), 568–579.
14. Hanfmann, E., and J. Kasanin. "A Method for the Study of Concept Formation," *Jour. Psychol.*, 3 (1937), 521.
15. Kasanin, J., and E. Hanfmann. "An Experimental Study of Concept Formation in Schizophrenia, I: Quantitative Analysis of the Results," *Amer. Jour. Psychiat.*, 95 (1938), 35.
16. Nadel, A. "A Qualitative Analysis of Behavior Following Cerebral Lesions," *Arch. Psychol.*, No. 224 (1938).
17. Storch, A. "The Primitive Archaic Forms of Inner Experiences and Thought in Schizophrenia," *Jour. Nerv. and Ment. Dis.*, Monogr. Ser., No. 36 (1924).
18. Vigotsky, L. "Thought in Schizophrenia," *Arch. Neurol. and Psychiat.*, 31 (1934), 1063.

See also Weigl, E. "Zur Psychologie sogenannter Abstractionsprozesse. I," *Zeitschr. f. Psychol.*, 103 (1927), 2–45; "II, Wiedererkennungsversuche mit Umrissfiguren," *ibid.*, p. 257.

DR. KASANIN:

In his article, Dr. Goldstein has pointed out the essential nature of intellectual disturbances of schizophrenic speech as revealed by his experimental method and he has also discussed the fact that in both organic cases and in schizophrenia there is fundamental change in the boundaries between figure and ground. In other words, there is a disappearance of the normal boundaries between the ego and the world, a sort of cosmic fusion which finds expression in many utterances and expressions of the patients.

Dr. Goldstein pointed out the difference between the schizophrenic's thinking and the thinking of a person afflicted with an organic brain disease. In addition to the extreme concreteness of the schizophrenic's thinking, there is the projection of his own ideas into his utterances and his performances. When given a task, he does it just as poorly as a man with a brain disease, but the schizophrenic's performance is more varied because his world is much larger and more animated than the world of the organic case. The schizophrenic animates things, embellishes them, toys with them, projects himself into them, and creates something quite different from the product of the ordinary performance of the injured brain.

The Disturbance of Conceptual Thinking in Schizophrenia

J. S. KASANIN, M.D.

IN 1930, on a trip to Russia, I became acquainted with the great Russian psychologist, Vigotsky, who was at that time in charge of the psychological laboratory of the Neurological Institute at Moscow and at the same time teaching psychology in the Moscow State University. He told me of his work with schizophrenics and asked me if I would like to be tested by a method which determined one's capacity for so-called conceptual thinking.

This was something new to me, and when I took the test I was amazed at its simplicity and at its great possibilities if applied to research in schizophrenia. I became quite well acquainted with the work of Vigotsky and of his co-worker, Luria, and subsequently Dr. Hanfmann and I have applied their technique in studying schizophrenic thought disorder.[1]

In the development of thought in the child there are usually three stages, which follow in natural succession. The first state is that of physiognomic thinking, in which the child animates objects and projects his ego into them.

[1] E. Hanfmann and J. Kasanin, "A Method for the Study of Concept Formation," *Jour. Psychol.*, 3 (1937), 521–540.

When the child plays with a stick and calls it a horse, we have an example of physiognomic thinking. This type of thinking is also called by Piaget "syncretic thinking."

As the child becomes older he develops a type of thinking which is called "concrete thinking" and which is realistic and literal. In this stage of thinking, when the child says "table" or "chair" he does not mean tables or chairs in general, but the particular table or chair which is in his house or which belongs to him. The thinking of most uneducated or undeveloped people is of this type. It is for this reason that people use various adjectives in describing objects; they have as yet no capacity for generalizations.

The capacity to use language to form abstractions and generalizations is something which comes quite late in the development of the individual, usually after adolescence, and probably with some education either formal or informal. This third type of thinking is called "abstract thinking" or "categorical thinking," and is a property of the educated adult person.

Vigotsky and Luria utilized a very simple method, developed originally by Ach, of using blocks of different sizes, shapes, and colors, which are easily classified in accordance with a certain principle requiring the formation and testing of several theories which the subject easily develops when he is asked to place the blocks in four different groups. The more elementary ways of classifying the blocks in accordance with color and shape usually do not work, and then, after several trials and errors, the right principle of classification is found, which usually does not take very much time or intellectual effort. The whole test involves the principle of inventing several theories and applying them, testing them to see if they are right or wrong. This capacity to form and test theories or concepts is evidence of the highest type of thinking. By this very simple method it is possible to learn if the person has the capacity, or has lost the capacity, of making theories and generalizations.

We have tried it on 62 schizophrenics, on 95 normal people, and on 24 cases of organic brain disease, and we have found that usually in schizophrenia there is a very definite reduction in this type of thinking.[2] It seems that the schizophrenic thinks largely in more concrete, realistic, matter-of-fact terms, in which things have a personal rather than a symbolic value. As Dr. Sullivan has indicated, language becomes the purely personal property of the schizophrenic. The schizophrenic is not able to grasp certain general principles or the idea of classification according to certain principles, and frequently develops other principles and other classifications than those which the average person adopts. Even more important is the fact that even when the principle upon which the classification is based is explained to the schizophrenic, he frequently refuses to use it and maintains his own classi-

[2] E. Hanfmann and J. Kasanin, *Conceptual Thinking in Schizophrenia* (New York, Nervous and Mental Disease Publishing Co., 1942). The materials for this test can be obtained from Stoelting & Co., 420 Homan Avenue, Chicago, Ill.

fication, for which no general principle can be adopted. He puts the most heterogeneous blocks together, stating that they belong together because they are "all policemen" or "all little people," although they are dissimilar in all aspects so far as can be seen by the normal person. It seems that the schizophrenic classifies his material under the purely physiognomic aspects of the material.

Another important fact is that the schizophrenic shows endless hesitancy and vacillation between various aspects of the material. This is due to his inability to abstract one principle of the given material while he neglects the others. He takes all the possibilities into simultaneous consideration, which of course makes it impossible to solve the problem. There is also a tremendous variability in the schizophrenic performance which is quite different from that found in organic cases. The performance level of the organic patients is not only lower than that of the normal controls; it falls even below that of the schizophrenic group and approaches the primitive level. The organic patients never understand the task as a classification, they never interpret a correction as proving to themselves that their attempts were wrong, and they never concern themselves with the totality of groupings. If they reach a solution of the problem, it is in a purely mechanical way, which is not what schizophrenics do. General paretics do much better than arteriosclerotics.

There is also a good deal of variability between patients, as the degree of intellectual impairment may vary from patient to patient. It is interesting that the organic patients never produce the artistic physiognomic groupings so prominent in the performance of schizophrenic patients. The schizophrenic vacillates between the various aspects of the test material; the organic case does not. A schizophrenic patient, when he starts to sort the blocks according to color, becomes attracted by the shape, and then does not know which way to turn or how to classify the blocks. The organic patients do not show this ambivalence. They are drawn by one or another aspect of the material and show no conflict or hesitation. Somehow the schizophrenic is more aware of the problem which the test presents, whereas the organic case goes about solving the problem in a cheerful, direct, and frequently incorrect manner without really comprehending the task involved. One great problem in all our work is not the fact that we find, in cases of schizophrenia, reduction in capacity to form theories, but the assurance that the patients had this capacity before.

In all our work we must be quite sure of the previous capacity of the patient to deal with abstractions and of his capacity to form generalizations. We feel that we are probably quite correct in postulating a reduction in the capacity to think abstractly in schizophrenics, but we are not sure about the fundamental tenet of our theory: that conceptual thinking develops at adolescence. We feel that a great deal more experimental work has to be done with adolescence and certain types of mental disease, especially organic cases, before we can come to this conclusion. In this respect, the work of Dr. Cameron has been extremely important since he has utilized our method and then checked with his own methods in cases of schizophrenia as well as in cases of organic brain disease.

In going over our schizophrenic material, we have been attempting to determine what clinical pictures are associated with definite impairment of conceptual thinking. We have classified our material on the basis of the total clinical picture which these cases presented. Our cases fell naturally into the following categories:

1. A group of the so-called "neurotic" schizophrenic cases in which there is a history of elaborate neurotic defenses erected by the patient in an attempt to solve his personal problems. Schizophrenic reaction comes here only as a last resort, when other neurotic defenses fail. These are the cases in which an unsuccessful attempt is made to overcome difficulties by developing a very clear clinical picture of either obsessive or hysterical neuroses with symptoms so prominent that the diagnosis of schizophrenia is somewhat in doubt. To this group also belong the cases in which there is a frank emotional conflict over certain instinctive drives which are unacceptable to the patient.

2. Cases showing marked dissociation with extensive compensatory fantastic elaboration, with primitive archaic ideas of omnipotence coming to the surface, with the feeling of a certain mission in life that has to be per-

formed, and with a variable regard of the ordinary realities of life.

3. Old cases of schizophrenia showing definite ideas of reference with delusions of persecution, associated with very little emotional reaction to these ideas. There is a general flatness in mood and some dilapidation, the sort of patients that one describes in hospital practice as somewhat deteriorated.

4. Acute episodic psychoses with marked overactivity, extreme dramatization of conflicts in a setting of fairly good contact with reality, and a tendency toward clear intervals. These cases would correspond partly to the catatonic cases, or the acute schizoaffective psychosis described in a previous communication.[3]

5. Cases in which there is a striking involvement of intellectual functions with marked incoherence and irrelevance, with tendency toward neologisms, "word salads," and peculiar syntactical speech formation; the type of case which originally gave the idea of intellectual involvement in schizophrenia. These cases are so clear-cut and so sharply differentiated that I take the liberty of calling them cases of "primary thought disorder."

In analysis of the material in terms of these five groups, it seems that the patients who show no impairment in thinking, at least as revealed by our methods, are patients in Group 1, in which the individual develops a psychosis

[3] J. Kasanin, "The Acute Schizoaffective Psychoses," *Amer. Jour. Psychiat.*, 13 (1933), 97.

as a culminating point in a series of attempted neurotic solutions of a basic maladjustment. In these cases the prognosis is not necessarily fatal. The reaction may be reversible. There is a reasonable doubt whether such cases are really schizophrenic, if that term is used in a sense of eventual deterioration. The problems which these patients present can be readily understood in terms of their special personalities and of the environmental stresses which they have experienced. These cases present so little distortion of the environment that one can readily understand them and seriously argue the existence of a psychosis. Also included in this group are cases with mild paranoid reaction, developed as the only way of dealing with a serious instinctive conflict.

The patients who show the most marked impairment in thought are those in Groups 3 and 5, that is, patients who are either flattened or dilapidated with evidence of social deterioration, or cases of primary thought disorder which I have described in Group 5. The patients in Group 4 may or may not show the reduction from conceptual thinking to more primitive types of thinking, depending upon the duration of symptoms and severity of attacks, and the degree of recovery between attacks. These are the cases which have the best chance of recovery with various forms of shock therapy or psychotherapy, and are the cases which have a natural tendency to get better even if left alone.

Although work with the levels of thinking embodying a genetic point of view is of fairly recent origin, and although the various groups are still somewhat crudely differentiated, it seems to me that we have stumbled upon the correct direction for understanding the reduction in intelligence which takes place in schizophrenia. Undoubtedly something does happen. It is impossible to talk the problem out of existence, and it is only by taking into consideration the genetic point of view that we are able to understand what does take place in the schizophrenic.

To Kurt Goldstein we owe the understanding that both the schizophrenic and the organic patients act on a much earlier level than the normal person with the same intelligence and social status. At times, attempts to differentiate between the schizophrenic and the organic cases lead us to points of view which may not be valid. As Dr. Hanfmann has pointed out, the similarity between the organic cases and the schizophrenics may not be due necessarily to the same cause, but may be merely a consequence of the fact that disintegration in the organism follows the same general rules regardless of the original cause of the disease.[4]

A final differential analysis of the thinking of schizophrenia was recently made by Dr. Cameron. His own discussion of his work, in which he used our method together with certain techniques of his own, follows.

[4] E. Hanfmann, "Analysis of the Thinking Disorder in a Case of Schizophrenia," *Arch. Neurol. and Psychiat.*, 41 (1939), 568–579.

Experimental Analysis of Schizophrenic Thinking

NORMAN CAMERON, PH.D., M.D.

INTRODUCTION

EVERYONE who begins to work with schizophrenic persons finds himself involved sooner or later in a very baffling situation. Although both he and the patient seem to be talking about the same thing, they are repeatedly missing each other's points. It becomes evident at once to the observer that something must have gone radically wrong with the schizophrenic's machinery of communication, although it is difficult to make out what the trouble is. With further contact, he will also realize that the schizophrenic seems to be arriving at interpretations which others cannot share, by logical methods that others cannot follow. He is forced to conclude that the trouble goes much deeper into the patient's life than a mere linguistic confusion would.

Ultimately one will find that the disorganized or scattered schizophrenic has somehow managed to get himself isolated from the common social environment. He has become unable any longer to share genuinely in the attitudes and perspectives of those around him, to take their roles when mutual misunderstanding arises, and so to be able to assume their point of view, grasp their difficulties, and modify his own behavior to meet them. On the other hand, his own asocial development has brought him to a point where no one else seems able to take his role and share his perspective, either. I have discussed elsewhere the effects of defective role-taking functions as *disarticulation* from the social group (3–6),[1] and related them to symbolic products of functional immaturity in normal adults (2) and to the asocial thinking of young children (1).

In order to clarify what follows, it is necessary to emphasize here the fact that it is quite impossible in human adults to separate thinking from language behavior. As the child gradually acquires speech the organization of his thinking slowly changes because of it; and since the organization of his language is determined by his social environment, his thinking tends to become progressively more socialized. The continual interchange between a given person and those around him not only develops the social character of his language and thought, but also maintains it afterward at an adequate social level. For if this organization falls below the point of intelligibility where others can share it, and if it cannot then be amplified by other words, gestures, signs, or demonstrations, it can no longer function in communication. As we shall see, that is just what happens in schizophrenic disorganization. Social communication is gradually crowded out by fantasy; and the fantasy itself, because of its nonparticipation

[1] Numbers in parentheses refer to References Cited on p. 63 below.

in and relation to action, becomes in turn less and less influenced by social patterns. The result is a progressive loss of organized thinking, and ultimately an incapacity for taking the role of others when this is necessary to enable one to share adequately in their attitudes and perspectives.

Experimental Studies

The studies which form the basis of this report were begun in an attempt to reduce the investigation of schizophrenic thought disorganization as nearly as possible to the conditions of an experiment. In order to have as homogeneous a group as possible, we used only patients with clinically unmistakable scattering, twenty-five in a logical problem (3, 4) and five, with severe scattering, in a manipulative sorting problem (6). The logical problem consisted of fifteen uncompleted sentences ending in *because* which were presented orally to each patient, who was allowed to complete them in his own way. A manipulative task was provided by the Hanfmann-Kasanin concept formation test (7) which requires one to make groupings of blocks on a double principle. This had the advantage of eliciting both verbal and nonverbal maneuvers simultaneously so that the experimenter could compare them. Everything that the patient and the experimenter said or did was recorded at the time in shorthand. Our analysis of these data showed as characteristic of schizophrenic disorganization:

Asyndetic Thinking.—This consisted in a marked paucity of genuinely causal links (*asyndesis*), both in the logical problem and in the sorting test. In place of well-knit sequences, which the situations demanded, the best our schizophrenics were able to do was to throw in a cluster of more or less related elements. There was convincing evidence that the patients felt these all to be related in some way, as indeed they usually were, but what they gave was only a half-organized collection of fragments instead of a functional unit. One of our patients, for example, when asked what caused the wind to blow, said it was "due to velocity, due to loss of air, evaporation of water . . . the contact of trees, of air in the trees" (3). Another completed the sentence, "I get warm when I run because . . ." with the following couplet, which he insisted upon writing down for us:

> Quickness, blood, heart of deer, length,
> Driven power, motorized cylinder, strength.

These solutions cannot be dismissed as either "irrelevant" or "incoherent," for they are certainly about the general subject and loosely related to one another. Neither are they nonsense or a "word salad," as such products are too often called. But still they are very poor material for a conversation. A normally syndetic, or linked-together, logical organization would have automatically eliminated all but one or two such possibilities, and in this way have restricted the solution to something more clean-cut and precise. This is what we find all through schizophrenic scattering—a lost ability to restrict, eliminate, and focus on the task in hand. The schizophrenic, you might say, is shooting at the target with a verbal shotgun where he should be sighting along a rifle.

Metonyms and Personal Idiom.—The *metonym* is an unprecise approximation in which some substitute term or phrase is given in place of the more exact one that a normal person might use. The result is analogous to what one gets in looking at something through steamed glasses. One patient says that he "has menu three times a day" instead of food or meals; another was "born a male sense" instead of just a male; a person's body "intervenes light" instead of intercepting it; fishes live in the water "because it's the natural resource of life" instead of "it's natural" or "their mode of life"; a patient upon resuming his task after a drink of water remarks, "Business walks as usual." Not just one but several of these may be strung along into sentences like, "A boy threw a stone at me to make an understanding between myself and the purpose of wrong-doing," and, "I was transferred due to work over here due to methodical change of environment." Taken in the frame of the individual patient's life and his known fantasies, these sentences can be translated into more precise, socially current forms.

It is this need for continual translation and sharpening of the focus that confuses and fatigues the listener. It gives the same feeling of strain that comes when one tries to follow a conversation in a foreign tongue with which one has some acquaintance but not quite enough. One goes along for a bit all right, but then begins to slip behind and miss the meaning. If one can write it all down, a good deal of it can be made out. The schizophrenic, of course, is not speaking in a foreign language; but he is speaking in an asocial dialect full of idioms that have value only for himself. He has fallen into this dialect in the course of growing more and more isolated from others.

It is often striking how well satisfied many of them are with their very inadequate communication, showing little or no evidence of concern over its unintelligibility. They either fail to recognize that you are having trouble or they are haughty about your stupidity. This fact is of prime importance. The patient evidently feels no need of doing anything about it for your benefit. He is no longer able to take your role in this situation, to put himself in your place and then speak more from that vantage point; and his own asocial patterns have reached a point where you are not able to take his role, either. This disorganization, in addition to being a result of growing isolation from social participation, is itself helping to accelerate the process and to perpetuate it by cutting off all effective communication by word of mouth.

Interpenetration of Themes.—When schizophrenic preoccupation reaches a point where it shuts out external influences, as if they were all intrusions, a new relationship develops. It is found only in severely disorganized and preoccupied individuals. One observes that the intrusive material—in our work the theme of the logical sentence—can neither replace the fantasying nor be completely excluded, as it might be in stupor. The resulting compromise is very interesting. On analysis one finds certain elements belonging to the external problem interspersed in the stream of preoccupation which it could not halt.

For example, a patient of mediocre intelligence has been preoccupied for years with fantasies in which he is a great engineer. All his talk shows it. He completes the sentence, "My hair is brown because . . ." with this, "Because it is a sort of hydraulic evering. (What does that mean?) It means that it gives you some sort of a *color blindness* because it works through the *roots of the hair* and hydrasee. . . . That is a study of the *growth of plants*, a sort of *human* barometer, hydraulic hydroscenic method." Ignoring the neologisms, which help to supply a pseudo-scientific terminology, one can see that the terms I have italicized are fragments of the intruding problem. They are not ordinarily present in his stream of talk. The two themes, that of the hair color and that of the still dominant fantasy, have interpenetrated with each other. Such a situation, in which a patient's asocial fantasy themes are able continuously to subordinate all external events in the field of social behavior, provides the patient with only a distorted and fragmented environment, which cannot possibly influence his conduct in a socially organized way.

Overinclusion.—In the sorting test, the chief reason for our patients' failure was their remarkable inability to maintain the boundaries of the problem and to restrict their operations within its limits. All sorts of objects from outside it were brought into the situation—the desk blotter, the telephone, the experimenter's pencil, wristwatch, and shirt, and even the walls of the room and a man outside the window. One patient said, "I've got to pick it out of the whole room. I can't confine it to this game" (5). His insight did not help him, however.

Things absent and out of the past were also brought into the task. No yellow men were working beside white ones in the hospital, therefore a yellow and a white block could not stand side by side. Personal conflicts intruded themselves. A woman patient could not bring herself to divide the blocks because for her this involved her separation from her husband and differences over having children; neither could she group them together, because, she said, "They belong together only if they are true." Another woman tried to solve the test as a means of "trying to figure some life out of the construction," etc. She got nowhere with it because she kept mixing into her manipulations questions from her already tangled personal life. These disorganized schizophrenics could not manage the essential first step in problem solving, that of narrowing down one's operations to something restricted and unified enough to call out organized attitudes and specific responses. Such a defect in organization has important implications for both the development and the perpetuation of clinical schizophrenia also (6).

Altering the Experimental Conditions.—Demands were made that the blocks be transformed in some way, that persons in the environment be changed before they could proceed, etc. A triangular block, one patient said, "needs a curve on it . . . a line for an axis," and "You have to swing a radius here, 3.1416, before you can do something with that" (hexagon). Another changed the position of blocks, "to get a different shape of the other." One decided to place a blue triangle with two red trapezoids, "because the colors blended and made it look a different shape" (6). It is suggested that this trend may be related to the patients' general inability to deal with facts as they are and to their tendency, when difficulties arise in the social field, to fall back upon some substitute in fantasy.

Incongruity between Acts and Words.—Patients who were attentively trying to solve the sorting problem often made statements about what they were looking at, or had just done, which grossly contradicted the perceptual pattern or the action. They made groups on the basis of color, and declared the principle to be that of form, and vice versa. Their manipulations might follow some common and obvious pattern; yet they characterized them according to a totally different plan, sometimes an opposite one (6). It was evident that their behavior disorganization permitted the coexistence of incongruous and even competing responses, in relation to the same things, without any tendencies toward fusion or compromise.

Generalizations Varied but Ineffectual.—In spite of the severity of their disorganization, our schizophrenic patients were able to set up numerous hypotheses, and to shift from one to another upon request without great difficulty (6). Their generalizations about what they had done or planned did not help them, however, because they were either too inclusive, too involved, or too much entangled with fantasy. Their formulations were often so disorganized that they apparently could not serve as adequate self-stimulation to aid them in their attempts at a solution.

Disorganization vs. Deterioration and Regression.—Considering the prevalence of certain contemporary attitudes toward schizophrenia, it was inevitable that in the course of this work two further questions should arise: *How does schizophrenic thinking compare with that in a known organic deterioration?* and *Is it regressive, in the sense of being childlike?* In order to meet these questions, the same logical problems were presented in the same manner to twenty-two deteriorated senile patients, twenty-nine normal children, and twenty normal adults (4, 5). Nothing comparable to the data we have been considering resulted in these groups of subjects. It may be concluded that, in this respect at least, the disorganized thinking of our schizophrenics followed neither the pattern of a common deterioration nor that of the normal child. It is quite true that the child is in the process of developing adult social language and thought organization, whereas the schizophrenic is in the process of losing it. But one process is not, as often erroneously implied, simply the reverse of the other. It is hardly more correct to assert that as the schizophrenic loses his adult organization he becomes a child in his thinking, than it is to say of normal children that as they grow up they recover from schizophrenia. We maintain that, in disorganizing, the schizophrenic develops a product that is new and unique in his life history (5).

Conclusions

It has already been intimated that organized adult language behavior and thinking are outgrowths of repeated social communication. Social communication depends upon the development of an ability to take the role of other persons, to be able to reproduce their attitudes in one's own responses, and so learn how to react to one's own behavior as others are reacting to it (1, 3, 4). The acquisition of this ability is what changes human organisms into social persons. Its loss, in one form or another, is the reason for the development of some of the most important phenomena in psychopathology.[2]

Every child is born into a predetermined social organization with a language system already in operation. While he is being inducted into his cultural pattern, he slowly acquires the prevailing system of communication as part of his own response repertory. His language behavior and his social thinking gradually take on the character of the speech and thought which he shares with those around

[2] This position has since been further developed in relation to defective role-taking in misunderstandings, delusions, and the formation of paranoid pseudo-communities. See Norman Cameron, "The Development of Paranoic Thinking," *Psychol. Rev.*, 50 (1943) : 219–233, and "The Paranoid Pseudo-Community," *Amer. Jour. Sociol.*, 49 (1943) : 32–38.

him; and by this means he develops the general attitudes and reactions of his group.

Among the latter, perhaps his most important achievement is that of learning to respond to his own behavior with the same attitudes and reactions which other persons show toward him. When he has succeeded in doing this he has acquired a second self, his *social self*. As he matures, this function should grow increasingly adequate. By it he learns how to be self-critical. When necessary, he can see himself as others see him, simply by taking their attitudes. He can then, if it seems good, modify his own conduct so as to fit himself better into the social pattern. If he cannot understand others, or they seem to miss his point, he can try to play their part for a while, take their role, and see how things look then.

Nothing else is so essential for the operation of this function, at an adult level, as language behavior and the social thinking derived from it. By their means a person can shift perspectives rapidly and easily on demand. If he finds his own attitudes are too far out of line with the others, he can then mend them in accordance with the roles he has just been assuming (2). His skill in this behavior will determine his social adequacy.

It is therefore no small matter when a person's language organization becomes disturbed in adult life. It means that he can no longer operate in communicative situations, that he cannot carry through social role-taking adequately, and consequently that he becomes unable to share the attitudes of others and to participate effectively in the life of his society. This is the plight of the disorganized schizophrenic.

Asocial schizophrenic adults always have a history of social inadequacy. If they have not been a problem to their family, their friends, or their school, they have usually been recognized as peculiar, detached, immature, "too quiet" or "too good." No one has as yet teased out all the factors responsible for their social ineptness; but its development seems always to go back to difficulties that long antedate the appearance of clinical symptoms. *It is our view that disorganized schizophrenics are persons who never have developed very adequate role-taking skills and have, therefore, not been able to establish themselves firmly in their cultural pattern.* In the face of emotional conflicts and disappointments, they find themselves unable to resist a progressive withdrawal from social participation into a fantasy life, into which they can carry their problems for solution or lose them entirely. At first, it may be, they merely decline to participate in the field of social behavior. But unless their growing fantasy life is broken into, its techniques will come in time to dominate all their activity and, as we have seen, ultimately replace their underdeveloped and now waning social skills, even in operations in the social field where they cannot possibly succeed. The characteristics that our experimental analysis has brought out are end stages in this process.

REFERENCES CITED

1. Cameron, N. "Individual and Social Factors in the Development of Graphic Symbolization," *Jour. Psychol.*, 5 (1938), 165–184.
2. Cameron, N. "Functional Immaturity in the Symbolization of Scientifically Trained Adults," *Jour. Psychol.*, 6 (1938), 161–175.
3. Cameron, N. "Reasoning, Regression and Communication in Schizophrenics," *Psychol. Monogr.*, No. 221 (1938).
4. Cameron, N. "A Study of Thinking in Senile Deterioration and Schizophrenic Disorganization," *Amer. Jour. Psychol.*, 51 (1938), 650–665.
5. Cameron, N. "Deterioration and Regression in Schizophrenic Thinking," *Jour. Abnor. and Soc. Psychol.*, 34 (1939), 265–270.
6. Cameron, N. "Schizophrenic Thinking in a Problem-Solving Situation," *Jour. Ment. Sci.*, 85 (1939), 1012–1035.
7. Hanfmann, E., and J. Kasanin. "A Method for the Study of Concept Formation." *Jour. Psychol.*, 3 (1937), 521–540.

DR. KASANIN:

In his contribution, Dr. Cameron discusses certain very important characteristics of schizophrenic thinking. According to him, the essential disturbance in schizophrenia lies in the social disarticulation of the patient, and this reflects itself in schizophrenic speech. The primary function of all language—communication—is gone. So far as content is concerned, it is quite a different story. The terms incoherence and irrelevance represent the reaction of the observer to the utterances of the schizophrenic rather than to careful analysis of the content as such. A special characteristic of schizophrenic speech is its extremely loose organization, the inability to select and eliminate, the tendency to approximate with injection of purely personal items in ordinary speech, described by Dr. Cameron as interpenetration. The same inaccuracies are found in the use of the familiar terms regression and deterioration. The child certainly does not show the same structure of language as a schizophrenic, so that regression becomes a very loose term, since the schizophrenic loses the adult organization of speech without acquiring a new one. In going further, Dr. Cameron points out that deteriorated senile patients do not possess the peculiar speech characteristics of schizophrenia, so that deterioration is also a very inaccurate term.

The next contribution is that of Dr. Benjamin, whose work is especially interesting since it gives us an analysis of schizophrenic thought disturbances as revealed by the Rorschach test. The results of this test check quite closely with those of his own method which consists of presentation of proverbs and fables, and solutions of logical problems.

A Method for Distinguishing and Evaluating Formal Thinking Disorders in Schizophrenia

JOHN D. BENJAMIN, M.D.

THE CONTENT of this communication is somewhat narrower in scope than the subject matter of the round-table discussion. Anomalies of language and thought in schizophrenia are so numerous, and apparently so varied in nature, that it seems methodologically sounder to choose one or more circumscribed groups of them for investigation than to lump them together in one category; after they have been thoroughly studied in this manner, it may be possible to see whether they can be brought under one heading, or whether we are dealing with a variety of mechanisms that differ fundamentally in their genesis and clinical significance.

A few types of so-called formal thinking disorders, then, have been the object of an as yet incomplete investigation over a period of years. Disturbances of language have been considered only secondarily, to the extent they have appeared as a result of the method of study employed. The important question of the justification of distinguishing between disturbances of thought and those of language, and between disorders of form and of content in both fields, is too complex to be considered in all its implications in a short discussion of this sort, although it will of necessity be briefly touched upon later.

Before describing the method used, a few words about the evolution of this particular investigation will perhaps serve to clarify and delimit some of the problems it is attempting to solve as well as to explain some of its biases and defects. In the course of a long-term study of schizophrenia the Rorschach test has been used extensively in conjunction with the clinical investigation of patients. Among the many uses to which the test can profitably be put in schizophrenic research is its particular suitability to the study of thinking disorders; as a matter of fact, almost all the "typically" schizophrenic Rorschach characteristics, those which permit a blind diagnosis to be made without necessarily referring to the content of the answers, are in the field of "thinking," or closely allied to it (succession, F plus per cent, DdW and DW, formally absurd Dd's, discrepancies between these and other factors). Without wishing at this time to go into any of the technical details involved in this aspect of the Rorschach investigations of schizophrenics, a few preliminary statements of results should be made. (1) *Not all schizophrenics show in their Rorschach tests those signs of intellectual malfunctioning which probably correspond to formal thinking disorders clinically*. Among those who do, there are of course marked quantitative and qualitative variations; but there are also some in whom there is a complete absence of these findings. (2) *Some, although not all, of these signs appear to be relatively independent of the stage of the illness and the momentary clinical condition of the patient.* They are, to be sure, found in almost all so-called deteriorated cases, but are also seen, sometimes in less pronounced form, at very early stages, occasionally long before a clinical diagnosis has been made, as well as after clinical recovery from a severe attack. This point deserves special emphasis because it is at variance with the findings of other authors, using different methods, that certain thinking disorders in schizophrenics could not be elicited in early or recovered cases. (3) *There appears to be a definite prognostic significance to these signs.* This statement requires considerable qualification. The evidence for it is of two sorts, direct and indirect. The former consists of clinical observation of the subsequent course of patients manifesting these signs, and is necessarily very incomplete since the investigation has been in progress only four years and is at present interrupted. Moreover, external circumstances have unfortunately prevented adequate follow-ups of most of the large number of patients tested. At the present stage of our investigation, then, this type of evidence has no statistical value whatever except that involved in the careful study of the small number of patients. So far as it goes, however, it seems to show that *only those cases with formal thinking disorders tend to "deteriorate," and that the severer these disorders are, the greater are the chances for, and the quicker the course of, the deterioration.* It is not implied, of course, that all or even the majority of these patients have "deteriorated," or will do so in the future; on the contrary, many of them have shown good remissions. In none of the cases examined personally by the writer, however, has there been a true psychiatric recovery without "schizophrenic defect." Some have already suffered a second, more severe, attack, and others undoubtedly will. We are thus dealing, if these findings are confirmed, with the "tendency to deteriorate," in the Bleulerian sense. Among cases with no Rorschach signs of formal thinking disorder, on the other hand, there are a few who have made apparently complete psychiatric recoveries to the level of the prepsychotic personality. Others in this relatively small group are still ill, in some cases better, in others unchanged, but presenting no evidence of affective or intellectual disintegration—that is, deterioration. I refer here to those well-organized paranoids verging on paranoics whose relationship to true paranoid schizophrenias is still a matter of doubt, and who seldom deteriorate in the usual sense of the word.

This brings us to the second type of evidence mentioned, the indirect, consisting of the appraisal of the various clinical states in which the Rorschach signs of thinking disorders are most frequently seen. Here the findings are clear-cut, although their absolute significance may well be questioned. The signs are found most consistently and pronouncedly in dementia simple (100 per cent), chronic insidious hebephrenia, chronic insidious catatonia (when a sufficient amount of test material is obtainable), and in those forms of so-called paranoid schizophrenia which are characterized by passivity feelings, delusions of influence, somatic hallucinations, and a strong subjective feeling of a changed personality. They are found less frequently and less severely, and are sometimes totally absent, in acute catatonics and paranoids without the above-mentioned symptoms, as well as in the chronic well-organized types. Disregarding the inadequacies of the usual classifications, it is well known that the first group has a much poorer natural prognosis than the second.

The importance of these findings, if they are confirmed through careful follow-up studies, is obvious. Clinically they have already proved useful. To give but one example out of many, several cases have made it possible to distinguish, with much greater certainty than is possible through clinical examinations alone, between those frequent adolescent schizophrenic-like reactions with ideas of reference and withdrawal and the prognostically entirely different insidious beginning of a deteriorative schizophrenia in adolescence, dementia praecox in the original Kraepelinian sense. Those familiar with the literature of Continental, and particularly German, psychiatry of the past two decades will doubtless already have been struck with the possible parallel between the observations offered here and the rather speculative but in part clinically founded concepts of many of these authors respecting the existence of at least two types of schizophrenia, concepts which have found expression in the opposition of "process schizophrenia," on the one hand, and "schizophrenic reaction," "schizophrenic state," "schizoid reaction," on the other. If further research should prove the working hypothesis as outlined here to be correct, namely, that there are schizophrenias with and without formal thinking disorders, irrespective of the severity and stage of the illness, this would perhaps constitute the best criterion for distinguishing between process and reaction. It must be borne in mind, however, that it is possible that the presence or absence of thinking disorders is a quantitative and not a qualitative difference, that their absence merely means that our methods of detecting them are too gross. This, if true, would in no way invalidate the prognostic significance of their quantitative differences. The implications of a *qualitative* difference, however, go far beyond prognosis. We have avoided the term process schizophrenia because its use in Continental psychiatry usually has involved the equating of process with endogenous-organic, and reaction with exogenous-psychogenic. That this assumption is premature in the present state of our knowledge of schizophrenia is clear. Perhaps it is true; perhaps not. But the demonstration of qualitative differences between two types of the illness, and a reliable method for distinguishing between them, would surely obligate the investigator in this field to consider the possibility of differences in etiology and pathogenesis, and to conduct his researches accordingly, whether these be along psychological or neurophysiological lines.

Of the many reasons which made it seem advisable to complement the Rorschach test with some other method in continuing these investigations, I shall mention only one, namely, the difficulty involved in translating the Rorschach findings into general psychological terms. The Rorschach test has proved an ideal instrument for distinguishing these disorders, and will, I believe, be equally valuable to investigations into their development and dynamics, but for purposes of exactly describing and delimiting them it is somewhat clumsy. It was mentioned previously, for instance, that some of the Rorschach signs of thinking disorders are largely independent of the clinical stage and severity of the illness, whereas others show marked dependence upon this factor. It is obviously of great importance to know what these signs represent in non-Rorschach terms, but the test alone cannot tell us this with certainty or clarity. For this and other reasons, then, a method was sought which would not only serve as a check upon the Rorschach findings, but which in itself would permit this one aspect of the investigation to be carried on with greater ease and simplicity.

The Method

The method—which, like the Rorschach, is not a test at all in the strict psychological use of the term—employs five means: a series of proverbs and phrases, simple logical problems, classifications of geometrical figures, repeating and finding the "moral" to a story, and solving a problem in ingenuity. The classification of geometrical figures, suggested by the method used by Weigl in studying cerebral lesions, has much in common with the investigations of Bolles and Goldstein, published since the commencement of this study two years ago. Because of time limitations, only the first means employed in the test, the interpretation of proverbs and phrases, will be discussed in the present communication.

Although the use of proverbs in intelligence testing is a well known and established practice, its application to the problem of schizophrenic thinking disorders is of comparatively recent date. Beringer, Gruhle, and particularly Hadlich (1931) utilized proverbs in their investigations of these disorders, and showed clearly that many schizophrenics have great difficulty in giving the meaning of a proverb correctly; no systematic working out of the material was undertaken, however, and no clinical correlations made. The choice of proverbs for our purposes was dictated by three factors: clinical experience of the frequency of disturbances in their interpretation; the belief that they would offer excellent opportunities for demonstrating the nature of some of the more typical thinking difficulties; and the fact that, if their systematic investigation should prove of value, they could easily be inserted in a routine formal mental-status examination.

The following fourteen proverbs and phrases are read

in the order given to the subject, who is asked to explain what they mean.

1) When the cat's away, the mice will play.
2) Don't cry over spilt milk.
3) It never rains but it pours.
4) The burnt child dreads the fire.
5) Don't cross your bridges till you come to them.
6) A rolling stone gathers no moss.
7) Discretion is the better part of valor.
8) To fiddle while Rome burns.
9) Don't count your chickens until they're hatched.
10) The proof of the pudding is in the eating.
11) He who laughs last, laughs best.
12) New brooms sweep clean.
13) Ingratitude, thy name is woman.
14) He travels swiftest who travels alone.

The examiner must make sure that the patient understands that he is supposed to "interpret" the proverbs and phrases. Before discussing their choice and sequence, I should like to give several examples of actual answers, and their analysis.

Patient A:

to (1) When there's nobody watching, they do things they wouldn't if the cat were there.
to (4) That should be sufficient warning not to go near the fire again.
to (8) Do nothing to put the fire out.

Patient B:

to (1) If there isn't any cat around, the mice will monkey around, and maybe get into things.

to (4) Once you get hurt, you want to leave fire alone.
to (10) If you're a good cook, people will like your cooking. The proof is when you eat it.
to (12) You can't get in the corners very well with an old broom.

At first glance, these literal answers will seem to many psychiatrists to be convincing evidence of mild mental deficiency, and to have no relation whatever to schizophrenia. Certainly there is nothing bizarre or fantastic about them, they display no weird symbolism, they are expressed in simple coherent language; they merely seem stupid—yet actually both of these patients tested slightly above normal during their psychoses. Although such answers are occasionally given by nonpsychotic individuals testing between 80 and 90 IQ, they are rare even at this level; yet they are common among schizophrenics, even highly intelligent ones, though frequently in somewhat less obvious form. For instance, Patient C, an intelligent college student, answered to (2), "After the milk has been spilt, it's too late to do anything about it anyway."

Patient D [IQ 138!]:

to (1) As applied to what? Just gives the mice more liberty.
to (3) It means nothing more nor less than extremely wet weather.
to (4) Simply a case where experience has taught that child that fire can burn him.
to (6) Just like comparing anything or any situation to a rolling stone—as long as it's in motion it isn't going to gather moss.

to (12) It means that the quality and also the quantity of any job that can be done with any product is better when new than if it has been used several thousand times.

In contrast, compare the following answers given by Patient E:

to (1) The last supper of Jesus, all those that kissed the novitia, the covitia. The political world is too much, we can't fight it, we can't see murder.
to (5) Don't cross your bridges until you come to them is right. It's true. Oh, mother; oh, mother.
to (6) A rolling stone gathers no moss—Christ. Breaking chain stores all together. Independency.
to (10) That's my pudding, doctor. All God give forgiveness. Oh, mamma, why did they make expensive weddings? Why don't they stay home, mamma?

Here we have productions that fulfill all the classic requirements of schizophrenic thought and speech: bizarre content, incoherence, peculiar sentence structure, obviously complex-determined sexual and religious preoccupations, a clang-determined neologism, and so on. As contributing to our knowledge of psychodynamics, such productions are undoubtedly more interesting than are the formal thinking disorders with which we are primarily concerned here, and are profitably subjected to a descriptive analysis of their formal structure and, whenever possible, to a psychodynamic study of the content. Yet these answers of Patient E are not germane to the immediate problem under consideration here, inasmuch as they constitute a "refusal" of the patient to undertake the given task, namely, the interpretation of the proverbs, and thus cannot be evaluated in terms of relative success or failure in this task. Incidentally, results of investigation thus far carried on show that content and form disorders of the sort displayed in these answers, while common in disturbed patients, disappear with improvement, and are not found in early or mild cases. Such answers must not be confused with others in which similar disturbances are combined with difficulties in interpretation. Thus, for example, to (1): "That means feline absence and rodential job, which has its sources in the nature of the Saviour; divine forgiveness, Heaven and Hell, inscrutability," where in addition to many obvious and typical schizophrenic features, which we shall not pause to analyze now, there is the same literal rendering of the proverb as in the answers of the first four patients.

Although they differ from one another in some minor respects, all the examples given thus far illustrate the highest possible degree of *literalness in the approach of the patient to the assigned task.* In order to emphasize the prevalence of this finding, to demonstrate the varying degrees in which it is manifested, and to exemplify some of the other most frequent response types, the answers given by twenty patients to the same proverb, "A rolling stone gathers no moss," are listed. It should be stressed that these patients vary in intelligence from normal to highly superior, in clinical condition from very early to advanced stages; symptomatologically all groups are included, with the exception that no extreme excitements or stupors are represented.

1. "A stone that keeps rolling doesn't stay still long enough to have moss grow on it."

   Complete literalness, marked *L* for purposes of a tentative semiquantitative scoring system being used for this one part of the test.

2. "It doesn't stay long enough in one place."

   Formally this answer is slightly different from the previous one, which was a restatement of the proverb with a connecting causal explanation of its literal meaning. Here the proverb itself is omitted and only the explanation given. The difference is surely not significant, however, the main point being that only the literal meaning is considered. *L.*

3. "Simply, that the speed of the stone would prohibit the gathering of any substance. You know, I feel that things have a tendency to stick to me, even with speed."

   L, formally identical with No. 2. This answer was given by a very intelligent young male schizophrenic after more than two years of hospitalization with no improvement.

4. "Anything that moves quickly doesn't allow anything to adhere to it."

   Again *L,* this time with a feeble attempt at a generalization from the specific example. Given by a young woman of superior intelligence during an excellent remission from a severe paranoid attack.

5. "A moving object is unsuitable for plant growth."

   The patient subsumes the specific instance cited in the proverb under a general statement. This pseudo abstraction, as it might well be called, is formally a *generalization from the literal.* Since it is quite common among intelligent schizophrenics, we mark it separately, as *GL,* although it is doubtful if its significance differs in any way from that of *L.*

These completely literal answers, while not pathognomonic for schizophrenia, are very typical of it, as stated before. They are not given by normals of average or higher intelligence. In deficients they are fairly common, although usually expressed somewhat differently, with less ease and assurance, and a greater attempt, even if unsuccessful, at interpretation. Thus a sixteen-year-old boy with an IQ of 68 replied, "That means we shouldn't be a rolling stone; it don't gather any moss." Here, in spite of the completely literal repetition of the proverb, there is some understanding of the rolling stone as having another meaning than its literal one. However, the outstanding fact is that these answers are *much more common in intelligent schizophrenics than in mildly defective nonschizophrenics.* The same consideration holds true for the organics, with the qualification that at present our test material in this group is too limited for adequate evaluation. Most of the organic patients tested did not include completely literal answers in their responses. One markedly deteriorated senile replied to (10), "If it tastes good, it ought to be all right, I guess." A twenty-three-year-old posthemorrhagic-encephalitic, testing 78 at the time of his hospitalization, answered, "Something that ain't still don't gather any moss, trying to tell us not to be a rolling stone," in close analogy to the reply of the defective boy quoted above. *Apart from organics, defectives, and a few borderline deficients, completely literal answers have not been elicited outside of the schizophrenic group.*

6. "Someone who is always rolling from one place to another will never be successful."
   Here the meaning is given fairly well, but the verbal expression is tinged with literalness (rolling). Marked *l*.
7. "If you just run around, you don't get any moss. That is, you get no money." *l*.
8. "People that don't stay put, don't gather anything." *l*.

The schizophrenic significance of these *l* answers is more difficult to evaluate. They occur frequently in mild deficients and occasionally in dull normals. One hypomanic gave a somewhat similar response. Within the schizophrenic group they occur more often at the lower intelligence levels. On the other hand, the fact that they do occur in schizophrenics of superior intelligence, often in conjunction with *L* responses to other proverbs, confirms their relationship, in some cases, to the latter. In the absence of any other signs of formal thinking disorder, their presence in the test of a schizophrenic could be interpreted in this direction only with great reservations and with particular reference to the intelligence of the patient.

9. "A person who brags all the time never gets anywhere."
   A totally different type of response, characterized by *false desymbolization,* and marked *FS.* The necessity for clarifying the term makes this an opportune time to discuss what steps are involved in the interpretation of a proverb.

The classic proverb, as represented on our list of fourteen by the first, second, fifth, sixth, ninth, tenth, and twelfth is built up of one or more substantive symbols, usually objects of nature or everyday life (cat and mice, milk, bridge, stone, chickens, pudding, broom), combined with predicates which have varying degrees of figurative or literal value (play, cry, cross, gather, count, eating, sweep clean). The literal meaning of the proverb can be a simple statement of real or supposed fact, sometimes based on observations in nature, at other times containing a cause-and-effect relationship (1, 4, 7). Or it may consist of a piece of homely advice (2, 9). In all cases, however, the objects as well as the actions are supposed to represent (symbolize) something else, the objects usually either types of human beings or more or less abstract categories (cat—person in authority, rolling stone—restless or changeable person, fire—unpleasant experience, spilt milk—past events). As long as no real interpretation is offered, this symbolization plays no role. The subject can refuse entirely to enter into the problem, whether from hostility, fear, preoccupation (Patient E), distractibility, or other causes. To be included among refusals are such playful responses as that given by a witty hypomanic to (1): "In other words, where the cat's a way, there's a will." On the level of complete literalness he can, as we have seen, repeat the proverb in other words, explain the logic of its literal meaning (Example 2), or generalize from the literal meaning (Example 5). Or he can dispute the truth of the statement, as did one patient in responding to (12): "I'm not sure that's correct," or even find fault with its logic, as in remarking upon (5): "That's ridiculous. How could you cross a bridge before you come to it?"

In order to make a true interpretation, however, the symbols must be translated into the respective figures, categories, and actions which they represent, a process which we have called, for the limited purpose of this inquiry, desymbolization. Following desymbolization, the meaning of the proverb can be expressed in various ways, from the most specific and concrete examples through the general to the abstract. The process of interpreting proverb (1), for instance, can be reconstructed schematically as follows: When the cat's away, the mice will play. After desymbolization: When the person in authority is away, those under his authority will play. Examples of expressions of this meaning, from our material, schizophrenics and controls: 1. "That means when the boss is away, the employees will have a good time." This highly concrete type of answer is quite common in normals of average and lower intelligence. 2. "When there's no one to watch, people do things they wouldn't otherwise." A general statement, getting away from the specific example. 3. "When authority is lacking, deportment is less restrained." A more abstract rendering of the meaning.

It need hardly be said that by this artificial reconstruction of the processes of interpretation we do not mean to imply that they actually occur separately and follow one another chronologically. On the contrary, all that is known about thinking would tend to prove that the problem is approached and solved as a whole. It is obvious, for instance, that a correct desymbolization can only take place if the meaning of the proverb is grasped at the same time. Nevertheless, in the investigation of defects in the process it is advantageous to consider its component parts, for purposes of classification of the faulty responses and comparison between schizophrenics and controls. It may well be that some of the differentiations we have provisionally made, not all of which will be discussed and illustrated here, may prove in the long run to be meaningless; others have already demonstrated their value, and we are perfectly willing to incur the reproach of pedantic overclassification in order to minimize the risk of overlooking essential differences.

We find disturbances of interpretation in respect to all the various part processes outlined above. Thus we speak of false desymbolization, false generalization, false abstraction, as well as oversymbolization and overabstraction. It is an interesting fact, previously noticed by several observers, that the schizophrenic who is most literal, who has the greatest difficulty in dealing with normal symbols and abstractions, often shows a predilection for unusual symbolism and pseudo-abstract thinking.

10. "Somebody who runs around, and does a lot of talking, doesn't get anywhere." *FS.*
11. "If you think about trouble, it'll pile up and become a mountain before you know it." *FS.*

Examples 9, 10, and 11 are all false desymbolizations and illustrate the great variety of answers of this type obtained. This is undoubtedly due to the fact that they are particularly adapted to the expression of individual, sometimes complex-determined, content, including psychotic preoccupations. For this reason they are difficult to evaluate in the sense of formal thinking disorder, although the study of their content can be most instructive. They are found in dull normals and mild defectives, but are much more common in schizophrenics, including those of higher intelligence. One response of this type was given by a depressive, another by a mild apathetic bromide delirium.

12. "That a person who is always busy doesn't stop for reflection, doesn't grow in mental and moral stature."

    A beautiful example of false desymbolization, this time unmistakably schizophrenic in quality owing to the equation of "gathering moss" with "growing in mental and moral stature," bordering on oversymbolization. The whole constitutes a piece of schizophrenic pseudo profundity.

13. "Well, that means a fellow that's ambitious, and keeps going, won't get stale."

    Although at first glance this also is a false desymbolization, it really belongs in a different category, and must be discussed because of its frequent occurrence in response to this particular proverb. Number (6) is the only proverb on the list (with the partial exception of 12) to which it is possible to give a second, almost diametrically opposite, but meaningful, interpretation without false desymbolization. 'A rolling stone' is a passable symbol for 'a fellow that keeps going'; and 'gathering moss' is certainly an excellent symbol for 'going stale,' as witness the word "mossback." In view of this, it might be expected that such an interpretation would be fairly common among normals; certainly there would be no a priori reason to expect to find it more frequently in schizophrenics, since no formal thinking disorder seems involved. Actually, however, it was given by very few nonschizophrenics, and was extremely common in the schizophrenic group, including some cases in which evidence of formal thinking disorders was lacking. In seeking a reason for this seeming paradox, the first question is why so few normals give this interpretation. Very probably the answer is that they have often heard the proverb used "correctly." [In a special study undertaken to determine the influence of familiarity or lack of familiarity with the proverbs upon their interpretation, some fifty of the subjects tested, both schizophrenics and controls, were questioned on their acquaintance with each of the proverbs and phrases. Number (6) was, with (2), the best known, familiar to all but one of the nonschizophrenics and to all the schizophrenics questioned. Significantly, the one normal who said that he had never heard the proverb was one of the very few who interpreted it in the sense under discussion.] In spite of equal familiarity with it, however, many schizophrenics give the unusual meaning. Several possible explanations of the phenomenon present themselves. It may be due to lack of contact with reality, with past experiences even in the intellectual field, unsatisfactorily vague as this concept is. Or, as is much more likely, in some cases it may be the expression of a negative emotional attitude, or of a desire to be different, to refuse to say the usual thing. In examining the following responses, however, one is struck by still another possibility:

14. "A person who is active will not let grass grow under his feet, and will get ahead."
15. "Be on your feet, and no grass will grow under them."
16. "A person standing still doesn't let any grass grow under him."
17. "Keep on the move, and don't let grass grow under your feet."

Seven other similar responses are contained in our material. Disregarding minor differences in their structure and logic, they are similar in respect to the inversion of the usual meaning and to the use of the expression "grass growing under your feet"; it is highly probable that the latter was the determining factor in their production. They exemplify a common finding among our schizophrenics, the tendency to interpret a proverb in terms of another proverb or figurative phrase. This "proverb" response, marked *P*, is, of course, not in itself evidence of faulty interpretation, but it usually is combined with it, as will be illustrated below. (The *P* response itself can provisionally best be understood as a manifestation of pseudo abstraction.) Here a fairly satisfactory *P* answer is made possible through the equating of moss with grass (i.e., a literal translation without desymbolization) and the inversion of the meaning. The literalness of this association was nicely illustrated by one patient who responded to every phrase with one word only; e.g., to "It never rains but it pours," with "Water." In answer to (6) he replied, "Grass." The formal notation for these answers is therefore *P– –l*.

18. "A loud mouth speaks an empty mind."
    A *false abstraction* marked *P– –FA*.
19. "Haste makes waste." *P– –FA*.
    These answers are typically schizophrenic, but again not pathognomonic, occurring occasionally also in unintelligent but intellectually ambitious normals.
20. "Dissipation of energy rather than concentration."
    Overabstraction, marked *OA*. The proverb is correctly understood (desymbolized), but the attempt to put its meaning in abstract terms overshoots the mark. While found in several schizophrenics, this type of answer can also be met with in moderately intelligent normals.

These examples should suffice to illustrate the more frequent types of disturbances found in interpretation. I have purposely omitted from this discussion responses in which content disorders are particularly noticeable, since these are usually more difficult to classify formally. Before leaving this proverb, however, I should like to cite two more examples. The first was given by an intelligent young man suffering from a postadolescent reaction which had been called schizophrenia. All tests failed to show any evidence of formal thinking disorders. His answer to (6) was, "Instability is nonproductive," which represents a satisfactory abstract response. The second, which will appeal to those of you who are by this time thoroughly sick of the various meanings assigned to our trite proverb, was given by the witty hypomanic quoted once before: "Yes, but travel broadens the mind."

The selection of the proverbs and phrases, and their sequence, was made with several factors in mind. In general, the proverbs become more difficult toward the end, culminating with (12), which is not only the most difficult to interpret, particularly in abstract terms, but also the least familiar. The repetition of idea in (5) and (9) was designed to elicit a type of schizophrenic *perseveration* seen particularly clearly in the Rorschach test. Numbers (13) and (14) were inserted, among other reasons, in the expectation that they would elicit obviously complex-determined responses more frequently than would the others. The 'misquoting' of (13) was purposeful, in order to elicit possible responses to what is, after all, an absurd statement. All these minor details have contributed to the interest of the study, and will be discussed in detail when the full results of this investigation are published. One other finding, however, is of greater importance for our present purposes. It will be noticed that the proverbs are interspersed with phrases (6, 7, 8, 11, and 13), and that these vary in nature. For instance, (6) and (8) must be desymbolized like proverbs, although showing essential differences from them; (7), (11), and (13), on the other hand, require no desymbolization, but either translation from more general to more specific terms, or a mere restatement in simpler language. The purpose of these phrases is to test the schizophrenic's capacity for shifting from one type of problem to another, and they have elicited interesting results. To a much greater degree than in nonschizophrenics, *the patient who, with difficulty, has just succeeded in getting away from the literal meaning of a proverb, often fails to return to the literal when it is called for.* As one example out of many, a response to (13): "Gratitude is a virtue, ingratitude a vice."

Some tentative results of one aspect of this investigation in its highly incomplete state have been given for what they are worth. During the past two years the test has been administered to 84 diagnosed schizophrenics, 12 clinically doubtful schizophrenics, 11 organics, 2 manics, 1 hypomanic, 7 depressives, 15 defectives, most of them mild, 6 children between ten and fourteen years old, and 31 normal and psychoneurotic adults, a total of 169 subjects. The majority of schizophrenics have not been followed up, and some of the more recent ones are unknown to the writer clinically, the tests having been administered by others. Twenty tests were given by a colleague, Dr. Romano, to schizophrenic patients in the course of a clinical follow-up study undertaken by him; the results have been most helpful in demonstrating that marked improvement is not accompanied by the disappearance of formal thinking disorders as judged by this method. In this respect, as in others, the investigation confirms and supplements the findings of the Rorschach, based on a considerably larger series, and outlined previously. Rorschach tests have been taken on 58 of the subjects to whom this method has been applied, with a high degree of correlation between the indices of formal thinking disorders.

The disadvantages of the proverb method are obvious, and need not be discussed here; to an appreciable degree they are offset by the simultaneous application of other techniques. One great advantage, hardly touched upon in this communication, lies in the opportunity to deal with the relation between form and content. We have avoided this tempting subject, along with other dynamic problems, because of our conviction that a demonstration of the existence, nature, and clinical significance of these disorders must precede speculations upon their causes, if these are ever to progress beyond the speculative stage. These problems will be discussed in detail in a future communication, based on the findings of this test and the Rorschach in conjunction with psychodynamic approaches.

DR. KASANIN:

The disturbance of thinking in schizophrenia as revealed by the Rorschach test coincides closely with results of the Concept Formation test. Dr. Benjamin has found that the most marked disturbances in conceptual thinking are found in hebephrenics, in paranoid schizophrenics, and in chronic insidious schizophrenics. He found least disturbance in paranoics and acute catatonics. Dr. Hanfmann and I have found most striking disturbances in hebephrenics, cases of paranoid schizophrenia, and those cases which we have described as "primary thought disorders" when the disturbances of thought and language are the most striking features of the case and are easily revealed even on casual psychiatric examination. We have found grave disturbance of conceptual thinking in cases of extensive fantastical elaboration with ideas of greatness, feelings of a special mission in the world, identification with cosmic forces, and so on. We found these disturbances least in questionable cases of schizophrenia and in the paranoid homosexual cases, as well as in acute catatonic and schizoaffective psychoses.

Besides giving information about the intellectual status of the schizophrenics, the Rorschach test tells us about the other aspects of their mental life. Rorschach test results tell us something about the creative life of our patients, of their preoccupations and the way schizophrenics perceive the outer world with its experiences. Such interpretations, however, can be made only by persons who are skilled in the understanding both of the normal structure of intellect and emotions and in the mild disturbances and fine deviations from normality which these patients present.

Such interpreters are rare, but we are fortunate in having a contribution from one of them, Dr. Beck. He gives us a precise picture of the disturbances of thought as revealed by the Rorschach test.

Errors in Perception and Fantasy in Schizophrenia

S. J. BECK, PH.D.

IN MY contribution to the subject of language and thought in schizophrenia, I am concerned not so much with the peculiar grammatical structure or the bizarre language expressions of these patients as with presenting some material throwing light from another angle on the problem of schizophrenic thinking. I want to discuss the processes of perception and active fantasy in this disease group.

Language and thinking are, after all, representatives of percepts and of images. They are shorthand symbols for much larger pictures; sometimes a word may stand for an entire conversation. The evidence I am offering is concerned with the relative roles of these two particular psychological activities in the schizophrenic's peculiar mental processes: (*a*) his perceptions, or rather errors in perception; (*b*) the active creative fantasy. This evidence has been culled from Rorschach test responses. The specific and important issue which this evidence raises is: are the strange productions of the schizophrenic fantasies conceived by his living in a world of his own creating? or are they simply mistakes, misapprehensions of real sense impressions?

The common attitude in writers on this subject is to interpret in terms of fantasy, without distinguishing between imagination in the sense of a newly created picture and what is in fact the misconstruction of a perception. A question you may legitimately ask is: what constitutes a fantasy? and what is just a mistake? It would take us much too far afield to try to etch out here the different activities involved in these two psychological experiences. There is a difference, however, and the nature of it will be seen in some of the Rorschach test responses I will cite. In this test, a free association experiment in which the stimuli are ten standardized, symmetrical but conventionally meaningless ink blots, we have an instrument eliciting both kinds of response: creative fantasy and error of perception. The responses I am using as illustrations were all obtained from one patient. The following are the clinical facts:

Patient.—A young man not quite eighteen years old; the second of three children.

Physical history.—Negative except that at the age of ten patient had whooping cough, bronchitis, loss of weight; questionable diagnosis of tuberculosis or some other long infection. Physical findings at time of admission negative except for a systolic heart murmur.

Intelligence and school history.—Early IQ of 83; never very bright; lost two years of school because of questionable tuberculosis. In first year of high school at time of admission to hospital.

Parents.—Father: Nervous, indecisive, unable to handle patient. Never a good provider. Mother: Too quiet and serious; suspicious of patient's and his younger sister's activities; children locked in room at night to keep them out of trouble.

Onset of illness.—On the Friday before admission the patient received a message ordering him, on religious grounds, not to go to school. Patient found a message in the Bible in Revelation concerning the divine purpose of his life. The purpose involved a fifteen-year-old girl; patient made her come through storm and rain to spend four hours with him. According to Revelation, patient would marry the girl in the Rose Bowl at Pasadena.

In the hospital the patient was quiet and coöperative, but kept to himself, seemed preoccupied, sitting with contented expression on his face. He moved his hands and feet in a restless manner, spoke willingly and frankly, but was easily distracted by accidental stimuli. Appeared happy and contented in believing he was Christ with a divine mission to fulfill.

Diagnostic impression.—Complete dissociation of personality and no disturbance affect. Mood, one hundred per cent neutral. Indifferent attitude toward everything he said or did. Had all kinds of delusions about his power and divine mission. All symptoms made a very definite picture of schizophrenia.

Diagnosis.—Dementia praecox, paranoid.

What happens to the patient's thinking as revealed by a Rorschach test? It must be emphasized that the stimulus presented in this test is, a priori, a meaningless one. The point of reference whereby we judge a Rorschach response is the inherent meaning or reality which a majority of healthy individuals ascribe to the whole figure or to details of it. This was the principle followed by Hermann Rorschach, the psychiatrist who devised the test, and by the investigators who have been continuing his approach. In doing so we are only following the procedure of life generally. An object is named or its use designated by the opinion of a culture group. When any member of that group deviates materially from the common understanding of a particular object or concept, he is, in the group's vernacular, "crazy." The Rorschach test in this way becomes a cross section of thinking representing the individual's reactions in life.

We know from a considerable background of collected and rubricked Rorschach experience what the reality is, or what the meanings are in these meaningless ink blots. The following are examples of what happens to the patient's thinking.

In figure I,[1] a detail commonly seen as a "wing" is called by the patient a "face of a clown." In figure II a detail commonly taken as a "butterfly" or "moth" is seen by the patient as "the devil." In figure III the patient sees a "lamb" where the healthy see a "bow tie" or "hair ribbon." In figure V, usually interpreted as "butterfly feelers," sometimes as "rabbit ears," the patient sees "spears." Figure VI shows certain tiny details which, when selected by the healthy, are seen as "flower petals" or "tips of wings"; the patient calls them "feet of adultery." In figure VII the usual response to the white-space figure is a "sphinx head"; patient's response is "a lion." In figure VIII two tiny details seen by the healthy as "small human figures" are seen by the patient as "two arrows pointing up to heaven." Or again, two details normally reacted to as "rocks," or "flower petals," and commonly enough as "cows' heads," are, according to the patient's reactions, "a face,—two faces of women looking up there"; then he

[1] Figures are not exhibited here.

instantly changes this response to "three persons,—God, the lamb—no, the wife, the princess, and the doctor." To figure IX the patient's response is "face of a woman." The detail is very commonly seen as "head or face of a man." But always a man, and frequently a specifically named individual, such as David Lloyd George or Josiah Royce. Our patient sees the human face but calls it "face of a woman." For the usual "octopus" or "spider" of figure X the patient sees a "serpent." A detail of figure X is often seen as a "dog" or "lion lying down"; our patient sees "two persons." To another figure commonly seen as "lion or dog rearing on its haunches" the patient's response is a "man is bowing his head over a woman."

All these responses of our patient are, in the technical language of the Rorschach method, F minus. This is only shorthand for showing that they represent a disregard for the true form of the stimulus, the true form being that which healthy people see in the same ink blot or detail of it. Our shorthand for these healthy responses, Rorschach's *gute Formen,* is F plus.

Our present concern is with F minus, the poor forms. We can obtain some clue as to the conditions that produce them from a qualitative inspection of many as they occur in different clinical pictures. In doing so we distinguish three varieties. One consists of simple errors. The patient just makes a mistake. Such among my cited examples was the "face of a clown" where "wing" is the healthy response, or our patient's "lion" for the commonly seen "sphinx." This variety of response in the Rorschach test is commonly given by the feeble-minded, but it is found also in manics, in patients with brain pathology, and in schizophrenics. Its nature, I repeat, is an error in perception. The patient either does not recognize the presented stimulus for what it is, or its outlines are to him blurred or vague, so he take things for other than what they are.

The second and third varieties of F minus both differ from the first in this important respect: a personal need seems to dictate the transformation of the perception. These more personal F minus varieties are still errors. The patient is looking at something, and calls it something it is not. But, unlike the feeble-minded, the patient has the endowment with which to know the object for what it is. His consciousness is not clouded as from a toxin or as in a delirium. By referring these responses to what we know of the patient from non-Rorschach sources we can usually trace the distortion to some sociobiologic drive in him. Among the examples cited in our eighteen-year-old sexually maladjusted boy were the several "women's faces" for which sundry and totally different percepts are the normal ones. So too is his seeing a "woman's face" where a man's face is the invariable healthy percept. The patient, you will remember, is preoccupied with masturbation. This preoccupation is, however, still at a relatively obvious level. The F minus it generates, while not different in kind, does differ in degree from the third variety. This one, also personal, reaches much farther into the depths of the personality. The relevance of the responses "feet of adultery," "arrows pointing to heaven," "the devil," "the serpent," "God, the lamb—no, the wife, the princess and the doctor," to the patient's frustrations, his conflicts over his search for strength in religion—the connecting line between these personal drives and his F minus is, I believe, clear. These are the three kinds of errors in perception which the Rorschach test discloses—the three varieties of F minus.

Campbell,[2] in one of his shorter papers, describes three classes of hallucinations, varying according to their personal value or significance to the patient. They are, first, the casual ones which "have no special relationship to personal interests, emotions or experience . . . [they] owe their origin to impersonal factors, organic or toxic." Second are those "determined in or by the special domestic or occupational interests of the patient, as in the familiar occupational delirium." Third, there is "an important group, [which] . . . are not extraneous or irrelevant sensory elements in the periphery of the personality, . . . but are closely related to intimate matters of great emotional value, such as thwarted ambitions, personal attachments, religious aspirations, sexual conflicts, painful memories."

These three kinds of hallucinations appear to have their parallels in the three kinds of F minus. In saying this, I do not mean to interpret F minus as an index to hallucina-

[2] C. Macfie Campbell, "Hallucinations: Their Nature and Significance," *Amer. Jour. Psychiat.*, 9 (1930), 607–618.

tory experience. I do think that the dynamics are the same behind both groups of phenomena. Taking my cue from Campbell, I am calling the three the impersonal F minus, the personal F minus, and the very personal F minus.

So far I have been roaming in the field of perception, that is, reaction to sense stimuli. Now I will turn to that other kind of mental activity which is so freely ascribed to schizophrenics, the active fantasy. I am referring here to that kind of expression which has totally transformed a deep, unconscious wish. The overt production does not in these instances resemble the content of the wished-for experience at all. The dream is such a production in its most obvious form. Art has been shown to be a transmutation of this same personal need. Clinical psychiatry, and more especially psychoanalysis, are daily gathering examples of this activity in their patients. In its essence this active fantasy is a manipulation of old percepts and images already in the patient's mental repertory. He moves his mental furniture around and creates something new. It is a unity which, as given, has not been seen by anyone before, although we recognize elements of it. And it may have the further value that, as a unit, it calls out a rich and joyous surge of feeling from us. Such is great art. We recognize it as that which we have always been feeling and wanting to express. The perceptual images, according to the experimental psychologist Titchener,[3]

[3] E. B. Titchener, *A Text-book of Psychology* (New York, Macmillan, 1924). See the chapter on "Memory and Imagination," esp. p. 424.

"undergo translation out of one sense-department, along the lines of least resistance to another, and reduction from explicit representation to symbolism. Reduction does not mean approximation to a type; what takes place is that a mere schema, or part aspect, or fragment of the complex comes to do shorthand service for the whole." In the Rorschach test, the response that represents this process—so we think—is the *Bewegung* or movement (M) response. We have examples from our patient: "two angels worshiping the devil"; "dancing girls and priests bowing down to them"; "two husky men guarding the hole which is the bottomless pit." This represents, so far as the Rorschach experiment is valid, two series of psychic processes: (1) The M response does the shorthand service Titchener speaks about, representing much more in the patient's experience than is present in the association he expresses. (2) It is his experiencing of a realized wish, an unconscious wish of course, and realized in the unconscious.

This is a lot to say for an ink blot. But I could not possibly go now into the problem of validation. I only ask you to go along with me to the extent of accepting the Rorschach claims, that the M, movement response, really represents experiences of active creative fantasy. You have already seen that F minus represents errors of perception. It follows then that we have in the Rorschach test an implement for investigating the schizophrenic's mental processes in respect to this important question: Do his peculiar constructions, and formulations, exist in the imagination? Or are they simple errors? blurred outlines around his percepts?

I will refer here to the results of an extensive Rorschach investigation, made in the Boston Psychopathic Hospital, which embraced sizable groups of schizophrenics and a somewhat more limited supply of controls. It is the findings in respect to F minus (perception inconsistent with reality) and M (the active fantasy) that, naturally, interest us here. What are these findings?

Without straining your attention on figures and decimal points stating averages, median, standard deviations, and so on (the study has already been reported),[4] I do want to focus your attention on facts in the figures. They are:

a) In producing M or movement responses, the schizophrenic does not excel his nonschizophrenic friend. On the contrary, the incidence of M was found higher in the controls. Nor is the difference a statistically significant one. The schizophrenics do not, in other words, distinguish themselves in the Rorschach test by more of this important M response; nor do they give startlingly fewer M. Translated into the comparatively simple language of the psychologist this means that schizophrenics as a group do not engaged in more fantasy activity than a group of nonschizophrenics. In either group one may find some individuals with much, and some with little, M, which would mean that some schizophrenics manifest very little, if any, of this experience capacity, as some healthy individuals are capable of a great amount of it. In itself the amount of M, of creative activity, is not a discriminative index serving as critical evidence in the direction of the diseased or of the healthy group.

b) Turning to the F, or form responses, the findings are beyond

[4] S. J. Beck, *Personality Structure in Schizophrenia* (New York, Nervous and Mental Disease Publishing Co., 1939).

any doubt. The schizophrenics fall sadly below the controls in their numbers of F plus, accurately perceived forms, that is, percepts having regard for reality. For the benefit of the statistically minded, the difference over the standard deviation of the difference was fully 11.1, a very high reliability.

Placing the two sets of results side by side, the conclusion is that the schizophrenic excels in his tendency to misconstrue the world that is presented, giving it a form and outline which the healthier do not see, rather than in a greater creative power or in a superior ability to transmute his experience into something new and richer. The error may be dictated by personal needs, and the evidence in many of these responses points strongly in this direction. It may be due to a mental asthenia, Janet's lowered psychological tension, as the responses in many cases resemble those given in conditions of lowered concentration; and then too, they occasionally resemble the simple inaccuracies of the feeble-minded, who just cannot know any better. Whatever the dynamics, they are inaccurate in their construction of their world in a significantly greater degree than the controls.

This is the light that the Rorschach experiment throws on the schizophrenic's thinking. To recapitulate: These patients have no monopoly on fantasy life. They do construe their perceived data inaccurately. Their nonpsychotic friends, taken by and large, do somewhat better in respect to fantasy. These controls are unequivocally better in apprehending the realities of their world. One wonders here whether the general belief in the schizophrenic profuse fantasy life is not due to confusing distortion with fantasy. Fantasy actually involves a *creating* of something totally new. The "Hermes" of Praxiteles or the "Winged Victory" were new creations in this sense. Ideal human forms sprung from the artists' minds. To be sure, some of the schizophrenics' misconstructions take on fantastic forms. But this is still not fantasy. It is inaccuracy. From the Rorschach test investigations we must conclude that poor apprehension of the presented real world is what chiefly distinguishes the schizophrenic's percepts and his thinking; that, and not living in the world of fantasy.

DR. KASANIN:

This is a very important contribution, for we have learned things about schizophrenia which we did not know before. Science consists in refinement of our knowledge, and in this sense our papers are of great value since they destroy many erroneous ideas about schizophrenia which we have cherished for years. All of us have felt for a long time that our ideas about the inner life of schizophrenics are extremely crude, if not incorrect. Dr. Cameron has pointed out that our stock descriptions of schizophrenic speech are incoherent, irrelevant, and probably not true. Some ideas are much harder to give up than others, and one of the most cherished ideas we have about schizophrenics is that they live in a world of very rich fantasy. Dr. Beck agrees that schizophrenics live in a world of fantasy, but the fantasies of the schizophrenics, according to him, do not amount to much, and the main problem in schizophrenia is not an overabundance of fantasy but a poor comprehension of the real world.

If the language of schizophrenia is not all chaos, if it can be studied in the terms of the total situation and the degree of isolation of the schizophrenic from the world in which he lives, then there must be some general laws or at least semblance of rules which the organization of schizophrenic thought and language follows. Dr. von Domarus will answer this question, since he has unusual preparation and training for this particular problem. After publishing his very important contributions on language and thought in schizophrenia, he became dissatisfied with his own limitations in the field of linguistics and logic as applied to organized speech and language. He spent several years at Yale, where he studied the laws of logic and linguistics as applied to the speech of ordinary people, and then he applied these laws to schizophrenics.

The Specific Laws of Logic in Schizophrenia

E. VON DOMARUS, M.D.

WHEN DR. KASANIN invited me to speak before you he asked me to elaborate on the specific laws of logic in schizophrenia.

Because this topic involves an investigation of the question of whether or not psychiatric phenomena may be understood as deviations from the norm, or must be regarded as independent thereof, it seems to be of essential interest.

We shall proceed by investigating first the specific laws of logic in schizophrenia, and we shall then see what general aspects they may have for psychiatry.

L. S. Vigotsky[1] in his profound study on thought and speech concluded that there are to be distinguished at least five phases of development of thought and speech: first, the mental cause, origin, spring, or motive, of thought and speech; second, thought itself; third, egocentric speech containing implicitly the subsequently explicit phases of development; fourth, inner speech or endophasy; fifth,

[1] L. S. Vigotsky, "Thought and Speech Psychiatry," *Jour. Biol. and Pathol. of Impersonal Relations,* Vol. 2, No. 1 (February, 1939). Translated from the Russian by Drs. Helen Kogan, Eugenia Hanfmann, and Jacob Kasanin.

outer speech, or, as one might say, exophasy. In connection with our present inquiry into the specific laws of logic in schizophrenia it will be of interest to see whether or not schizophrenic thought and speech productions substantiate such a schema.

Whenever we feel a deficiency we concomitantly feel the wish to overcome it, especially if we are socially minded. Judging from the behavior of higher mammals, we should assume this to be true also of them. It has been pointed out elsewhere[2] that animals express by means of certain motions their feelings not only about conditions present, but also conditions desired. The latter they do by executing the motions they would make if their desires were fulfilled.[3] They behave as they would if their wants were actually being satisfied.

Before trying to show that mental defectives as well as highly deteriorated schizophrenics express themselves by motions of an as-if character, an example taken from the animal kingdom may help to illustrate this primordial phase of thought and language.

An elephant in a zoölogical garden, wishing to obtain a piece of sugar from a visitor, may be observed to go through the motions he would make had the piece of sugar already been obtained. He moves his trunk up and against the spectator, he plays with the snout as if grasping a piece

[2] E. von Domarus, "Zur Entstehung und Psychologie der Sprache," *Ann. d. Philos.*, Bd. 4 (1924).

[3] Hans Vaihinger, *Die Philosophie des Als-Ob* (Leipzig, 1920).

of sugar, and he may move his trunk toward his mouth as if throwing a piece of sugar into it. All these motions are naturally understood as expressing the wish to obtain food from his visitors.

On the other hand, a mute and mentally defective patient was observed to express her wish to eat by pointing at food, then by motioning with arms and hands toward her mouth, and finally by making chewing motions as if she had already been permitted to eat. When this same patient wanted rugs flattened out on the floor, she also went through the motions she would make if she had to flatten out a rug in reality.

Lastly, a highly deteriorated schizophrenic patient who once spoke but had not done so for many years, ran her fingers through her hair when she saw an attendant, and the attendant correctly inferred from such an as-if motion that the patient thus expressed a wish to be combed. This schizophrenic patient, as did the mental defective, asked for food by going through the motions she would make if she had already obtained food. She pointed to it, put her fingers into her mouth, and licked them.

The significance of these and similar observations lies in the probable correctness of the assumption that the physical or mental defective phase of as-if expressions is ever so often repeated during the process of schizophrenic deterioration of thought and language, indicating that the thought and language of schizophrenics may be in the nature of an atavism.

With this idea in mind let us now turn to illustrations of so-called specifically schizophrenic disturbances of logic.

Dr. Karl Birnbaum pointed out one day an unusual schizophrenic patient at the Herzberge Insane Asylum of Berlin. This patient uttered so-called nonsensical phrases; however, it had become evident that certain symbols, numbers, and relations which recurred might yield a degree of intelligibility, because the patient was willing to explain herself as best she could.

To the patient, each letter of the alphabet possessed a numerical significance according to its position; A equaled one, B equaled two, and so on. Occasionally, peculiar thought processes entered as a disturbing factor. For example, one should expect I to equal nine, and J, ten; but the patient insisted that J equaled nine, and I, ten. She explained that God (*Gott*) is pronounced like "Jot" in Berlin slang, and therefore, to avoid blasphemy, preceded I with J.

This patient produced many more illustrations of this type of schizophrenic thinking. With the assistance of Doctor Samuel Yochelson some of these have been translated, and a few of them will be given here. They reveal one of the fundamental laws of schizophrenic thinking.

For this patient, the number nineteen was equal to, or identical with, an Insane Asylum. She explained this peculiar statement in the following way.

19=Insane Asylum (*Irren-anstalt*), abbreviated J A, reversed A J. A J = 19. Therefore, 19 = J A = Insane Asylum. Why did she reverse J A into A J? Well, she said, A J means, in Polish, "yes"; but in German the word for "yes" is *ja*. Hence, Insane Asylum = J A = German "yes" = Polish "yes" = A J = 19.

21 = Bathing Station, 21 = 12. 12 means the twelfth month, and the twelfth month is the end of the year, but one bathes at the end of the year (and the new year is no longer the old or the reverse of the old year); hence, 21 = Bathing Station.

25 = Friedrich Wilhelm Hospital. After twenty-five years of service, war invalids go to the Friedrich Wilhelm Hospital. Hence, Friedrich Wilhelm Hospital = 25.

26 = Servant Wages. Twenty-six is the end of the ordinary alphabet, although patient adds to the letter z = 26 an extra letter, tz = 27. When the servant's wages arrived, it denoted the end of servitude. For example, the patient says: "When I wanted to work on the farm I received my wages for having served as a housemaid, and the receipt of wages indicated the end of work as a house servant." Hence, servant wages = 26.

27 = Old Age Pension. Tz = 27, the very last letter in the alphabet. The alphabet is at its end. When in certain years the two-day Christmas celebration happens to end on a Saturday, the 26th of December, there is also no work on the 27th, the latter day being a Sunday in this particular circumstance. When an extra day of rest occurs on the 27th, it is a relief to the aged. Relief to the aged is equivalent to receiving a pension, that is, relief to the aged = pension. Hence, 27 = Old Age Pension.

Let us consider one more illustration of this type of schizophrenic thinking. A schizophrenic patient of the Insane Asylum of the University in Bonn believed that Jesus, cigar boxes, and sex were identical. How did he arrive at that strange belief? Investigation revealed that the missing link for the connection between Jesus, cigar box, and sex was supplied by the idea of being encircled. In the opinion of this patient the head of Jesus, as of a saint, is encircled by a halo, the package of cigars by the tax band, and the woman by the sex glance of the man.

Apparently, our patient had the feeling that a saint, cigar package, and sexual life were identical; that is, the feelings which he experienced when he spoke of a saint, cigar package, or sex life were the same. Though an adult, mature person has never such a feeling of identity, it is to be noted that even for a normal person these so strangely unified objects have one particular in common. Were this not so, the schizophrenic could never be understood.

On the other hand, the difference between normal and schizophrenic thinking seems to be that, whereas for a normal person the particular of being encircled is only one of many accidentals, for the schizophrenic patient it is the quality expressing essence.

We are now prepared to discuss the illustrations of schizophrenic reasoning in respect to formal properties.

In its most precise form our logical thinking follows the so-called Mode of Barbara. If, in the figure, area A designates 'All men are mortal' and area B 'Socrates is a man,' then we conclude correctly that 'Socrates is mortal.'

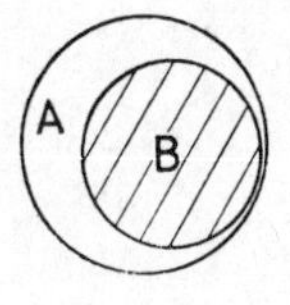

From the figure it follows at once that the last statement yields no new knowledge. To the concept 'man' belongs by implication also the man Socrates, and hence, simply by definition, as it were, Socrates is mortal.

Experience shows that the conclusion is justified only if the major premise implicitly contains the minor premise. If thinking does not take this into consideration, we arrive at what seems to be contrary to, or other than, normal thinking, or to be paralogical.

An arbitrarily selected illustration, with the aid of the following figure, will elucidate the nature of paralogical thinking.

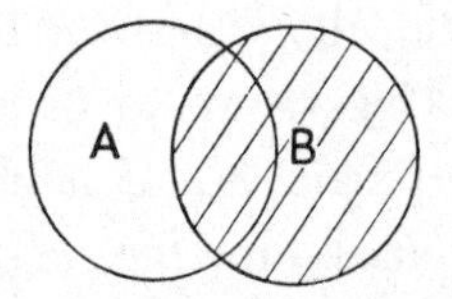

If A means 'Certain Indians are swift' and B means 'Stags are swift,' the area of intersection of A and B symbolizes the common element of swiftness.

It follows for the paralogical thinker that 'Certain Indians are stags,' and he will act as his conclusion directs him to do. A glance at the figure reveals a further, most important point. Because everything which lies outside the common intersection of A and B is irrelevant for the identification of A and B, the law of contradiction is excluded from paralogical thinking and its paragrammatical language.

Thus the above-mentioned patient asserted that a saint and a cigar box were identical because they were identified as surrounded. Neither the nature of the 'surroundings' nor that of the 'surrounded' made any difference in the conclusion drawn. The same mode of syllogistic reasoning also identified a saint and a cigar box with the male sex.

The difference between logical and paralogical thinking may be stated: whereas the logician accepts only the Mode of Barbara, or one of its modifications, as basis for valid conclusions, the paralogician concludes identity from the similar nature of adjectives. This idea might have been expressed by Vigotsky as follows: whereas the logician accepts identity only upon the basis of identical subjects, the paralogician accepts identity based upon identical predicates.[4] In the logical example the identical concept was the subject man, and Socrates was mortal because he was a man. In the paralogical example concerning the identity of certain Indians and stags, the identification was made from what may be said about them, that is, from a common single predicate. Furthermore, when a schizophrenic patient identified a saint with a cigar box and the male sex, he did so because of what he could predicate upon each one of these different subjects; and, because this predicate was the same for the three subjects, they were held to be identical. Upon examination the same kind of reasoning may be found reappearing in all other examples of paralogical reasoning.

[4] Vigotsky calls the subject of a sentence that about which something is said, and the predicate that which expresses what is said about the subject; subject and predicate are for him psychological, not grammatical terms.

We are now in a position to evaluate Vigotsky's discoveries. We have seen that he distinguished five phases of thought and speech. The phase antecedent to the final phases of esophasy and endophasy was the so-called egocentric speech. In egocentric speech inner and outer speech are not yet separated. The inner speech proceeds by thinking in predicates rather than in subject-predicate sentences; but I just stated that the paralogical thinker finds identity of subjects whenever and wherever he finds identity of predicables. The paralogician expresses himself in egocentric speech habits, for his thinking is predicative and he has regressed to the egocentric speech of the child. We know that the child's speech has some elements of the speech of primitive peoples. Therefore we are once more driven to the conclusion that the specific paralogical thought and speech processes of the schizophrenic are in essence those of primitive peoples. When the patient deteriorates still further, he acquires modes of expressing himself which are still more primordial. An illustration of such a regression to an animal-like behavior is the as-if language and concomitant thought production. At the beginning of this discussion such production was exposed as atavistic.

The discussion set as its task to investigate first the specific laws of logic in schizophrenia, and then to see what general aspects the laws of logic may have for psychiatry.

The specific laws of language in schizophrenia show that they are the same as those of primitive people, or even those of higher animals. Of course, just as a decerebrized man does not become a fish, because the evolution and development of a cerebral cortex subsequently changed to a greater or lesser degree the function and structure of the entire central nervous system, so the regressive schizophrenic process does not make the patient a primitive. The patient exhibits only to a pathological degree some of the peculiarities of a primitive. It is this that makes it possible to understand in principle the laws of logic in schizophrenia as products of psychology, although of primitive rather than of adult psychology. It is the latter which makes it difficult, if not impossible, for an inexperienced adult to grasp the meaning of schizophrenic language; on the other hand, a scrutinizing study makes it possible, at least in favorable circumstances, to understand schizophrenic thought processes as deviations from a norm rather than to conclude that they are independent thereof. The general aspect of the laws of logic in schizophrenia seems to indicate that thought and language in schizophrenia are chapters in psychiatry.

DR. KASANIN:

Dr. von Domarus has given us an excellent review of what is now held to be the classical position in reference to disturbance of schizophrenic thought. It is quite obvious that the problem of language in schizophrenia will not be solved until the same thorough study is applied here as to so-called normal speech. It seems to me that since the problem is so difficult the very best minds in the fields of logic and philosophy should be attracted by the study of language in schizophrenia. There is the obvious difficulty, however, that scientists dealing with these problems know very little about psychiatry. Fortunately, however, Dr. Angyal has investigated the disturbance of thought in schizophrenia as a logician and a philosopher; some of the conclusions and results of his research are discussed in the next article.

Disturbances of Thinking in Schizophrenia

ANDRAS ANGYAL, M.D.

IN REVIEWING the literature on schizophrenic thought disturbances one finds that the various authors are for the most part in agreement on the phenomenology of these thought disturbances. Divergences of opinion exist mainly with respect to the interpretation of the facts. Most of the theories which have been advanced grasp correctly certain aspects of the problem, but none of them does justice to all the facts which have been gathered on this topic.

I wish to indicate tentatively the general direction in which a unified theory of the various aspects of schizophrenic thinking disturbance may be sought. To this end a brief excursion into the field of logic must be made. The principal category with which natural science operates is that of relationship. However, as soon as we turn to the study of personality, of the total organism, or of any sort of whole or *Gestalt*, the concept of relationship seems quite inadequate for the description of the organization of these wholes. It has been frequently pointed out that *Gestalts* cannot be resolved into relationships between parts. The whole is neither a collection of parts nor a collection of relationships between the parts. The whole has a definite organization according to some unitary plan. I have previously described a category which seems to me well adapted for the logical presentation of holistic organizations.[1] I called this a "system-connection" or simply "system."

Relations and systems differ from each other in various respects. A relationship involves only two members, (1) the *relata* and (2) specific connections between them. Complex relationships can always be resolved into pairs of *relata*. Systems, on the other hand, may involve an indefinite number of constituents. The point needs no further elaboration, since I shall not refer to this aspect in the following discussion. Another characteristic of systems, however, has much relevance to what I am going to say. Systems are patterns—specific kinds of *arrangements of parts according to some unitary plan within a "dimensional medium."* This means that some sort of dimensional medium, some sort of field, is a *conditio sine qua non* for holistic organizations. The most common dimensional media are space and time, although they are by no means the only ones. We speak, for instance, about the vertical structure or depth of personality. This has no relation to space, but can still justly be called a dimension. For example, logical order between sub- and superordinate concepts represents also an organization in a dimensional medium. Any field or realm which permits a multiplicity

[1] Andras Angyal, "The Structure of Wholes," *Philosophy of Science*, Vol. 6, No. 1 (January, 1939).

of parts and in which parts can be arranged into patterns can be called a dimensional medium.

Another characteristic of systems should also be mentioned. The parts of a system are not connected directly among themselves, but are united in and by the whole. Furthermore, a part participates in the whole not so much through its individual quantities as through the *position* which it occupies in the total organization.

With this introduction I wish to advance the hypothesis that *the thinking of the schizophrenic patient is not impaired so far as apprehending of relationships is concerned; the schizophrenic*—when he fails in the solution of an intellectual task—*fails in the apprehension of system-connections.* I shall advance some arguments in favor of this hypothesis and then indicate briefly what the relationship between thinking disturbance and the rest of the schizophrenic symptomatology may be.

Wegrocki, in an unpublished study,[2] presented to schizophrenic patients groups of four words, only three of which belonged to the same category. The patient had to cross out the word which did not fit. An example of such a group of words is: cabbage–carrots–potatoes–meat. The patients very frequently failed on such a task, that is, they failed to find for the three words (cabbage, carrots, and potatoes) the more general concept, namely vegetable, and to exclude one of the four words, that is, meat, as one not belonging to that category. One may say that the

[2] H. J. Wegrocki, " 'Generalizing Ability' in Schizophrenia" (MS).

patient's ability to generalize, to find the superordinate concept, was at fault. I would formulate this somewhat differently. A class concept may be regarded as a field into which certain objects fall and others do not. The single objects are subordinated to the general concept, but otherwise the field has little structure and it may be said to represent a poorly articulated whole. Some other tests which are used for the examination of thinking presuppose a similar type of intellectual process, but the task is somewhat more complicated. For instance, in the Ach-Sakharov test one also has to find the general field or realm to which the individual blocks belong, but this realm is defined by a combined criterion of height and size.

The obvious objection may be raised that nothing is accomplished by reformulating these thinking disturbances into a new phraseology describing them as the inability to apprehend or constitute realms or fields to which a group of objects belong, or by calling the disturbance a difficulty in placing individual items in their corresponding fields. This type of disturbance can be adequately described in terms which are already in use, such as difficulty in concept formation, in abstraction, in generalizing, or in categorical thinking.

In order to point out certain advantages of the hypothesis which I have proposed, I wish to mention examples of a somewhat different type. You are all acquainted with schizophrenic writings which are abundantly interspersed with drawings. These drawings usually are not illustrations of the text but a continuous presentation of what the patient wants to express. This would indicate that the patient's intellectual activity does not stay within a unitary realm, but rather that he drifts freely from one semantic stratum into another. A peculiarity such as this can hardly be considered as an impairment of generalizing ability.

One of Bychowski's[3] patients, when asked where her husband was, answered that he was on the wedding picture. Here the realm of reality and the realm of representation are not kept apart. The facility of the schizophrenic in separating the realms of reality and imagination is notoriously impaired. Contrary to so-called normal thinking, which has to keep within the same realm or frame of reference or universe of discourse, the thinking of the schizophrenic is subject to little determining influence from the unitary field.

In an experiment on picture completion Hanfmann[4] found that "the common characteristic of incongruous placements is the disregard of the spatial relationships which are constitutive for a realistic pictorial representation." She further states that the totality of spatial relationships "yields a definite frame of reference for the objects and makes the picture a representation of a section

[3] G. Bychowski, "Certain Problems of Schizophrenia in the Light of Cerebral Pathology," *Jour. Nerv. and Ment. Dis.*, 81 (1935), 280–298.

[4] E. Hanfmann, "Thought Disturbances in Schizophrenia as Revealed by Performance in a Picture Completion Test," *Jour. Abnor. and Soc. Psychol.*, 34 (1939), 248.

of real space, that is, a space that contains objects governed by the laws of gravitation." When such a frame of reference is lacking, entirely incongruous elements may be brought together by the patient. This is quite in agreement with the view I am trying to express. Without giving any further examples, I think that one is justified in saying that in the realm of intellectual operations there are certain dimensional media. We may call them fields or realms or frames of reference or context or universes of discourse or strata. Some such field is necessarily implied in any system or holistic organization. The schizophrenic thinking disturbance is characterized by a difficulty in apprehending and constructing such organized fields.

Normally a person carrying out an intellectual task remains in the same field. This attitude is technically called a "set." Thus we may also say that the schizophrenic, in his thinking, fails to maintain and change the sets in an orderly way. Unexpected changes of sets always strike one as strange. For example, certain types of jokes are based on such a change of set or a "going out of the field." A joke mentioned by Freud is a good example of an unexpected change of set. A dealer in the Viennese horse market praises a horse to a prospective buyer: "If you start out from here at eight o'clock on this horse, you will be in Pressburg at eleven." Whereupon the customer answers, "What would I do in Pressburg at eleven o'clock?" Here is a jump from the realm of the hypothetical into that of the real. Such shifts from one realm into another are very frequent with schizophrenics, and therefore the patients' statements sometimes strike one as witticisms.

The fact that schizophrenics often produce what one calls an absurdity and often fail to recognize it as such is also explicable on the basis of the hypothesis which has been offered. We call absurd that which is out of place, incongruous, does not fit into the general context.

The lack of a clear separation between various fields which intermingle among one another also makes understandable the occurrence of those loose cluster formations and interpenetrations which have been emphasized by Cameron[5] as characteristic for schizophrenic thinking.

Much more extensive study is needed for testing the hypothesis that, in schizophrenia, thinking in terms of system is impaired, but not thinking in terms of relationship. I wish only to show here that the schizophrenic is from the beginning greatly handicapped in apprehending, creating, and manipulating clearly separated fields which are prerequisites for any system formation.

As I mentioned before, I mean by the term "system" the logical formulation of the type of structure or integration or organization which exists in wholes. Thus the schizophrenic thinking disturbance is a form of faulty integration. Very similar kinds of difficulties of integration characterize not only the thinking but also other aspects of the schizophrenic disorder.

[5] N. Cameron, "Reasoning, Regression and Communication in Schizophrenics," *Psychol. Monogr.*, No. 221 (1938), p. 34.

In closing my discussion I wish to touch briefly upon a problem which seems to me very important in this connection: the relationship between disturbances of thinking and the general nature of the schizophrenic disorder. We infer the presence of a thinking disturbance from the patient's verbal productions or from such nonverbal performances as imply thinking. A faulty end result in any performance may be due either to a defect in the tool or to a defect in using the tool. Thus, for instance, blindness may be due to a pathological process in the eye or in the optic tracts or in the calcarina—defects in the tool—or the defect may be in the person who uses the tool, as in victims of hysterical blindness. If we apply this distinction to our problem, we may ask, Is the patient's thinking mechanism, as such, impaired, or is he using an otherwise intact tool in an incorrect way because of certain difficulties in the broader aspects of the personality organization? I have the impression that most authors tacitly assume that the schizophrenic thinking disturbance represents a defect in the tool. Delusions result in faulty intellectual productions and still are not included among the thinking disturbances. The implication of this is that the delusion is an incorrect way of using one's thinking processes, and that the thought disturbance proper represents an impairment in the thinking mechanism as such. This implication, however, can hardly be justified. We may put the problem also in this way: Does the disintegration proceed from the periphery to the center, or vice versa? Is a kind of molar dissociation in the broader aspects of the individual's tendencies, wishes, fears, system of values, the primary fact, and disorganization of part function secondary; or vice versa? Weighing the available evidence for these two possibilities, there is little doubt in my mind that the disturbance starts in the broader aspects of the personality adjustment and, if the process is not arrested, proceeds to a molecular disintegration of part functions. The exact nature of the process which brings about the transition of a molar splitting to a molecular fragmentation cannot yet be clearly stated. I feel that future research might profitably be directed toward the investigation of the process of transition.

DR. KASANIN:

Dr. Angyal's contribution is an especially important one. He points out that the schizophrenics suffer not so much from difficulty in understanding relationships as from the fact that they fail to see connections in a unitary system in terms of which normal people speak and think. Hence, as has been emphasized by others, fact and fancy, background and figure, become mixed. He also points out that we all, somewhat naïvely, assume that a schizophrenic is really all right and that only his language and thought are confused. In other words, we have assumed that there exists a fault in the use of the tool; it is, however, of crucial importance to note that Dr. Angyal considers that the tool itself is damaged, that the personality disorder is primary and disturbance of thought and language is secondary.

Concluding Remarks

J. S. KASANIN, M.D.

ALL OF US have approached the problem of language and thought in schizophrenia from different points of view, using our own techniques, and it is indeed significant that our conclusions coincide so closely.

Schizophrenia, irrespective of its origin, will always remain, as pointed out by Vigotsky, a psychological problem, and it is fortunate that his approach is rapidly gaining favor. At times I have been discouraged by the fact that so very little research has been done in the field of the intellectual disturbances of schizophrenia; but when one compares the papers of today with the papers of Gruhle, Kurt, Schneider, Storch, or even Bleuler, we can easily see that we can formulate the disturbances of language and thinking in schizophrenia with much greater precision.

I shall now take the liberty of summarizing the various contributions and the discussions under their several headings, so that we can clarify what we have learned thus far and outline in what other directions our researches must follow.

First, we must differentiate to some degree between thinking and language, and, for our purposes, we shall assume that language represents external manifestations of thought. Like thought, language has its own laws as well as its special aims and, although by and large one is an aspect of the other, sometimes it is desirable to separate the two.

In the first place, what is the essence of the disturbances of schizophrenic thinking? Almost every paper here presented touches on the subject. We have the observations by Goldstein that in both organic cases and in schizophrenia there is a reduction of capacity in categorical or conceptual thinking as a result of which the patient lives in a world of concrete reality devoid of much general unity. Thinking is reduced to primitive, elemental, "concrete" performance which corresponds to simplicity and superficiality of behavior. Such things as fellowship, unity, and a sense of harmony, which are all attributes of man's conception of the universe, are not integrated, and man begins to live in a state of isolation. That is a great tragedy, involving all patients who suffer from a disease of the central nervous system.

My own work, which was done in coöperation with Dr. Hanfmann, confirms the same view as that of Dr. Goldstein, with the greater emphasis on schizophrenia. A schizophrenic cannot abstract one principle while he neglects others. He takes all possibilities into simultaneous consideration, which makes it impossible for him to solve a problem. We find again and again the lack of capacity to make generalizations. We also confirm with Goldstein the disappearance of the normal boundary between the ego and the world, which reflects itself experimentally in the loss of the differential between "the figure and the background," of the object and its background. For example, in the picture by Da Vinci the schizophrenic may not be able to separate the "Mona Lisa" from the landscape.

Benjamin points out the literalness of schizophrenic thinking. Thus, to the schizophrenic who is asked to comment on the proverb, "A rolling stone gathers no moss," it means exactly what it says; that a stone which rolls around doesn't offer a chance for moss to grow on it. The schizophrenic refuses to understand symbols, although he may use them a great deal in his own speech. Angyal points out that any holistic organization is really a system. Systems are patterns with parts arranged in accordance with some principle. A schizophrenic is aware of relationships, but he is not aware of system connections. Thus, a schizophrenic would put in the same class things which do not fit together. Again we have the realm of reality versus the realm of imagination; or the same problem of the ego and the outside world. There is no such thing as a single frame of reference or unity of a field. Shifting from one realm to another is characteristic of a schizophrenic. For example, I asked a patient why she was so unhappy. Her answer was that over her bed there hung Dürer's "Melancholia" and the picture depressed her very much. I suggested that she take the picture down, to which she replied, "If I do, I'll be it." In the same way, as noted by Bychowski, a woman, asked where her husband was, said he was in the picture.

Dr. von Domarus characterizes the thinking disorders of schizophrenia from a purely formal point of view. He points out that in schizophrenia you have paralogical rather than logical thinking. In formal logic we use the so-called Mode of Barbara. In this mode, the minor premise must be contained within the major premise for the conclusion to be true. Thus, when you say that all men are mortal and that Socrates is a man, he must be mortal too. The schizophrenic, on the other hand, makes conclusions on the basis of casual associations of objects. Thus, Indians are stags because they are as swift as stags.

Now that we have crystallized to some degree the disturbances of thought in schizophrenia, I should like to formulate more precisely the disturbances in language. Sullivan points out that the schizophrenic uses language to give him a sense of security in a world of strangers whom he does not understand, who do not understand him, and of whom he is afraid. The main function of language is communication. When people know each other very well and are intimate with each other, their speech becomes very simple and frequently limited to few words. In that sense it becomes autistic. People who feel close to each other use certain words and expressions which carry a great deal of meaning to them but which may be quite meaningless to others. All this takes place when the individual has a great sense of security with others; but when his security with others is impaired, the language is not used for communication and something else takes place. The language becomes individualistic, eccentric, and contains in it elements of magic. Things happen in the world of thought which do not happen in the world of reality. Because a schizophrenic has given up hope of communication with others, he uses language to counteract his sense of insecurity. Language becomes on the one hand very elemental, but on the other, odd, eccentric—"magic." The process of communication depends upon a feeling that when you say something the person who listens to you feels and thinks the same way you do and that you understand each other. Sullivan calls this consensual validation. It is lacking in schizophrenia. A schizophrenic speaks to bolster his own feeble sense of security like the man who talks loudly in the dark, trying to drown out his anxiety by the sound of his own voice. These disturbances in language are not necessarily an evidence of regression. The disturbances of language are essentially evidences of the disturbance in the function of communication which is the cardinal problem in schizophrenia. One wonders whether in schizophrenia the disturbances of language and thought are the effect of schizophrenia or the cause of it. Angyal puts it very well when he states that the disturbance starts in the broader aspects of the personality adjustment and, if the process is not arrested, proceeds to a molecular disintegration of part functions. We know also that when one produces experimentally, as in brain injuries, disturbances of the speech apparatus or any interference with the motor verbal process, the patient becomes angry and in every way tries to compensate for the defect in verbal expression by trying to communicate his thoughts to you in some other way. The schizophrenic, on the other hand, has no intention of changing his highly individual method of communication and seems to enjoy the fact that you do not understand him. The function of communication is the most important function of all and is the last thing to go. The patient may be very ill and greatly confused and yet be able to conduct some sort of conversation with his family and friends. It is when a definite, formal thinking disorder becomes apparent that prognosis becomes ominous. This has been brought out by Benjamin, and also by me.

In my own work, I have pointed out that patients with so-called primary thought disorders are the ones who show the signs of greatest deterioration and are less inclined to get well. It is in these cases that the capacity for communication seems greatly impaired. Cameron points out that schizophrenic language is neither irrelevant nor incoherent. If one takes the trouble to understand the patient, his experiences, and his difficulties, one will understand his speech. The difficulty is that his speech lacks unity and synthesis. The products are loosely connected into clusters of words, so that one is impressed by a certain diffusion of thought. There is a tendency to use inexact words, approximations, and the patient constantly interjects into his speech and language words and sentences which have a great deal to do with his own personal problems but nothing to do with the subject at hand. A schizophrenic does not regress to the level of childhood. He develops something new and unique: uses many substitutions, approximate phrases, and terms with highly personal idioms which make his language extremely difficult to follow.

The third question which has been raised in this discussion is the cause of the language impairment. This probably springs from an inability to know what is real and what is false. The whole field of reality testing has a very poor start in the preschizophrenic child. Because the child is not sure of the love of his parents he has a great deal of insecurity, he is not sure of himself, of his judgment and of the world around him. It is quite possible that very early in life the preschizophrenic child has not developed, or could not develop, a sense of differentiation between himself and the world, between what is true and false, between reality and fantasy. As pointed out previously, the schizophrenic is not able to make generalizations. He does not separate the object from the background. He does not take a definite attitude toward the world. Both Sullivan and Cameron emphasize the striking disarticulation from the social context. When a person suffers from interference in communication with his fellow men, he becomes isolated. Language then becomes highly individualistic and idiomatic. The schizophrenic becomes so used to his own language that he is no longer able to tell people what he thinks, even when he feels like doing so. One naturally wonders what the forces are which hinder the communication between the schizophrenic and the people around him. One also knows that one of the cardinal features of schizophrenia is ambivalence, which goes with incapacity to make decisions. This incapacity to make decisions is, in my opinion, due to refusal of the patient to make conclusions. To some degree this is also true of the neurotic. In many respects the schizophrenic is like a child: he is anxious to learn, to know, and somehow he does not succeed. A schizophrenic often speaks of his psychosis and the hospital as some sort of educational process, as a school, or as an experiment. A schizophrenic is afraid to know and afraid to learn. Whatever decisions he makes must be impulsive and instantaneous. That is the reason why suicides in schizophrenia are entirely unpredictable.

Coming back to the same problem, we find certain great difficulties which the schizophrenic has in relationship to the outside world. There is a failure or a fear to learn, generalize, and make definite conclusions. It is for this reason that a schizophrenic shows great tendency toward literalness in his thinking. It is also a defense against his own ambivalent tendencies. The patient avoids the necessity of making a choice. He accepts things as they are, he refuses to see the other side of the subject, he refuses to recognize symbols, and for these reasons appears somewhat childish; and, of course, the extreme docility and passivity of the schizophrenic patient spring from the same source.

The final topic concerns our old idea that schizophrenics spend a great deal of time in fantasy. If a schizophrenic is really afraid of his ambivalent tendencies, one would not expect too much fantasy, and this seems to be the case. Beck finds that there is no such thing as a rich fantasy life in schizophrenia. On the contrary, fantasy life is constricted and not expanded. The patients who spend years in bed do not have a rich fantasy life; they may have grotesque ideas and fantasies, but these are mere distortions. The schizophrenic patient, like the obsessive neurotic, is not creative. He does not transmit his experiences into something new and rich, but misconstrues the world as presented.

This entire presentation has been extremely valuable to us, but it raises many more questions than it answers. If in schizophrenia there has been a marked reduction in the capacity for conceptual thinking, one wonders why there is so little conceptual thinking among people in general. What is the relationship of conceptual thinking to intelligence, and how far does it depend upon our culture? The Russian psychologist, Luria, interested me in the whole subject of conceptual thinking. In 1932 he organized a psychological expedition into Central Asia, where there had been a very rapid industrialization of extremely primitive nomadic tribes. He showed that, because of their industrialization, there has been a marked advancement of conceptual thinking. We should like to know more about it in our own culture. We still do not exactly understand the differences between organic psychoses and schizophrenia. Thus far, Goldstein is the only one who has done work in this field, and his contributions are very valuable. We all agree that the most important cause of disturbances in the thought and language of schizophrenia is the disarticulation of the patient from his social context. Our main investigation should be in the direction of learning why and how it develops. It is quite obvious that early in childhood the child or the infant goes through some traumatic process which interferes with his relationship to the outside world. Everything becomes impaired and distorted: relationships to people, work, play, creative instincts, psychosexual development, language and thought. We know already a great deal, and we can describe quite well the "formal thought disorder" in schizophrenia. Our efforts now should be directed into the more mysterious field of early ego development and of the functions of reality testing in the preschizophrenic child.

Norton Paperbacks

PSYCHIATRY AND PSYCHOLOGY

Adorno, T. W. et al. *The Authoritarian Personality.*
Alexander, Franz. *Fundamentals of Psychoanalysis.*
Alexander, Franz. *Psychosomatic Medicine.*
Bruner, Jerome S. *The Relevance of Education.*
Bruner, Jerome S. *Toward a Theory of Instruction.*
Cannon, Walter B. *The Wisdom of the Body.*
Erikson, Erik H. *Childhood and Society.*
Erikson, Erik H. *Gandhi's Truth.*
Erikson, Erik H. *Identity: Youth and Crisis.*
Erikson, Erik H. *Insight and Responsibility.*
Erikson, Erik H. *Young Man Luther.*
Ferenczi, Sandor. *Thalassa: A Theory of Genitality.*
Field, M. J. *Search for Security: An Ethno-Psychiatric Study of Rural Ghana.*
Freud, Sigmund. *An Autobiographical Study.*
Freud, Sigmund: *Beyond the Pleasure Principle.*
Freud, Sigmund. *Civilization and its Discontents.*
Freud, Sigmund. *The Ego and the Id.*
Freud, Sigmund. *Group Psychology and the Analysis of the Ego.*
Freud, Sigmund. *Jokes and Their Relation to the Unconscious.*
Freud, Sigmund. *Leonardo da Vinci and a Memory of His Childhood.*
Freud, Sigmund. *New Introductory Lectures on Psychoanalysis.*
Freud, Sigmund. *On Dreams.*
Freud, Sigmund. *On the History of the Psycho-Analytic Movement.*
Freud, Sigmund. *An Outline of Psycho-Analysis Rev. Ed.*
Freud, Sigmund. *The Problem of Anxiety.*
Freud, Sigmund. *The Psychopathology of Everyday Life.*
Freud, Sigmund. *The Question of Lay Analysis.*
Freud, Sigmund. *Totem and Taboo.*
Horney, Karen (Ed.) *Are You Considering Psychoanalysis?*
Horney, Karen. *Feminine Psychology.*
Horney, Karen. *Neurosis and Human Growth.*
Horney, Karen. *The Neurotic Personality of Our Time.*
Horney, Karen. *New Ways in Psychoanalysis.*
Horney, Karen. *Our Inner Conflicts.*
Horney, Karen. *Self-Analysis.*
Inhelder, Bärbel and Jean Piaget. *The Early Growth of Logic in the Child.*
James, William. *Talks to Teachers.*
Kasanin, J. S. *Language and Thought in Schizophrenia.*
Kelly, George A. *A Theory of Personality.*
Klein, Melanie and Joan Riviere. *Love, Hate and Reparation.*
Levy, David M. *Maternal Overprotection.*
Lifton, Robert Jay. *Thought Reform and the Psychology of Totalism.*

Piaget, Jean. *The Child's Conception of Number.*
Piaget, Jean. *Genetic Epistemology.*
Piaget, Jean. *The Origins of Intelligence in Children.*
Piaget, Jean. *Play, Dreams and Imitation in Childhood.*
Piaget, Jean and Bärbel Inhelder. *The Child's Conception of Space.*
Piers, Gerhart and Milton B. Singer. *Shame and Guilt.*
Ruesch, Jurgen. *Disturbed Communication.*
Ruesch, Jurgen. *Therapeutic Communication.*
Ruesch, Jurgen and Gregory Bateson. *Communication: The Social Matrix of Psychiatry.*
Schein, Edgar et al. *Coercive Persuasion.*
Sullivan, Harry Stack. *Clinical Studies in Psychiatry.*
Sullivan, Harry Stack. *Conceptions of Modern Psychiatry.*
Sullivan, Harry Stack. *The Fusion of Psychiatry and Social Science.*
Sullivan, Harry Stack. *The Interpersonal Theory of Psychiatry.*
Sullivan, Harry Stack. *The Psychiatric Interview.*
Sullivan, Harry Stack. *Schizophrenia as a Human Process.*
Walter, W. Grey. *The Living Brain.*
Watson, John B. *Behaviorism.*
Wheelis, Allen. *The Quest for Identity.*
Zilboorg, Gregory. *A History of Medical Psychology.*

Liveright Paperbacks

Balint, Michael. *Problems of Human Pleasure and Behavior.*
Bauer, Bernhard A. *Woman and Love.*
Bergler, Edmund. *Curable and Incurable Neurotics: Problems of "Neurotic" versus "Malignant" Psychic Masochism.*
Bergler, Edmund. *Parents Not Guilty of Their Children's Neuroses.*
Coles, Robert et al. *Drugs and Youth: Medical, Psychiatric, and Legal Facts.*
Dewey, John. *The Sources of a Science of Education.*
Dunlap, Knight. *Habits: Their Making and Unmaking.*
Featherstone, Joseph. *Schools Where Children Learn.*
Gutheil, Emil A. *The Handbook of Dream Analysis.*
Gutheil, Emil A. *Music and Your Emotions.*
Jones, Ernest. *On the Nightmare.*
Köhler, Wolfgang. *Dynamics in Psychology.*
Köhler, Wolfgang. *Gestalt Psychology.*
Köhler, Wolfgang. *The Selected Papers of Wolfgang Köhler.*
Russell, Bertrand. *Education and the Good Life.*
Stekel, Wilhelm. *Impotence in the Male.*
Stekel, Wilhelm. *Sexual Aberrations: The Phenomena of Fetishism in Relation to Sex.*